HEDGEROW HARVEST

HEDGEROW HARVEST

Traditional Recipes from Nature's Storehouse

JAN ORCHARD

The Crowood Press

First published in 1988 by
The Crowood Press
Ramsbury, Marlborough,
Wiltshire SN8 2HE

British Library Cataloguing in Publication Data

Orchard, Jan
    The hedgerow harvest.
    1. Food. Dishes using edible plants.
    Recipes
    I. Title
    641.6'5

    ISBN 1 85223 098 3

Line illustrations by Sharon Perks

Typeset by Qualitext Typesetting Abingdon
Printed in Great Britain by Billing & Sons Ltd, Worcester.

CONTENTS

INTRODUCTION

I spent my childhood in a tiny Cumbrian village called Asby. There was no shop, no electricity, no school or church and very few buses. Instead we had the freedom to roam the fields and woods around us. We fished in the beck and picked blackberries, nuts, rosehips and sloes in their season, following a pattern set by generations of children before us.

I suppose that compared to other children in the 1950s we were rather a primitive lot. Nevertheless, when one thinks of the stresses and anxieties which face children today, we were incredibly lucky. I was more fortunate than most; my grandmother and my aunt lived only a few doors away and took me on expeditions to collect wood, mushrooms, wild strawberries or whatever was in season, and to visit their cronies, who all had tales to tell and knowledge to pass on. My mother was a great baker, who thought to her dying day that bought cake was a matter for shame. My father, although he worked in the high-tech world of Sellafield, was a great believer in keeping up old traditions. Even in remote Asby, we were one of the few families who still ate herb pudding at Easter and carling peas on Carling Sunday.

My friend Liz and I would roam an area which must have stretched at least ten miles, usually accompanied by my faithful terrier, Timmy. It never occurred to our parents to warn us against strangers or lifts in cars. Strangers were infrequent so a matter for curiosity, and never went unobserved; cars were rarer still.

Progressive agriculture was unknown in those days. The hedges and grass verges flourished uncut. Hay was still the main cattle food crop, so the fields were full of meadow flowers. Sadly all this changed in the 1960s when hedges were bulldozed and flower-free silage replaced hay. Asby itself changed beyond belief. Ugly new houses now blocked the view of the mountains from my aunt's house; the old ladies who generated such a sense of community and passed on the country lore from their own childhoods were all gone, replaced by young families who 'kept themselves to themselves'. My enduring memory of the old Asby is that cottage doors were always open and everyone knew everyone else, their business and their family tree. Today villages like Asby are quite different. I hope this book will help to bring back some of that old world.

Many of the plants and flowers I took for granted as a child are now so rare that they must not be picked. There is a 'country code' that we must all now follow, so when gathering berries, herbs or any hedgerow food, please, please remember the following:

- Don't tresspass.
- Close gates behind you.
- Don't uproot anything.
- Equip yourself with a good wild flower and plant identification book and don't touch anything rare or anything which you are uncertain about.
- Keep dogs under control.
- Never pick flowers, leaves or berries from a nature reserve or other conservation area.

You can also help to save Britain's declining wild flower population by creating a 'country corner' in your own garden. Most of the big seed companies have a wild flower collection. Many of the flowers will attract butterflies, bees and birds. Berries, such as rowan and hawthorn, provide winter food for thrushes and blackbirds. Creating such a garden is a good way of repaying nature for the abundance of good things it can provide in its own hedgerow harvest.

CHAPTER 1

FLOWERS AND LEAVES

BUTTERBURR

Butterburr is sometimes called bog rhubarb, probably because of its enormous leaves which resemble those of cultivated rhubarb. Farmers' wives used to wrap butter in these leaves – hence the name. It was a favourite remedy for heart diseases and was supplied by medieval herbalists; the famous Culpeper called it 'a great preserver of the heart and cheerer of the vital spirits'. The root was used to kill tapeworms, a common problem before meat was killed under today's hygienic conditions. One of the old ladies in my village, who was a great folk healer, used a poultice of butterburr leaves for bruises and sprains. Other medical uses were for treating coughs and fevers, healing wounds, curing stammering and relief of cramps. It has no real culinary value.

CAMOMILE

Camomile is one of the most useful of herbs. Although it is now widely cultivated it can still be found growing wild and is easy to recognise because it has small white ox-eye daisy-like flowers and gives off a strong, sweet scent, rather like apples.

Camomile is called manzanilla in Spain and is used to flavour sherry of the same name. A hair rinse, made from camomile flowers and leaves bruised and soaked in hot water, and soothing, relaxing camomile tea are both old remedies. Folklore says that camomile is a strong plant which will help others growing nearby to thrive, so many gardeners include it in the herbaceous border. Consumptives used to be made to sit near a bed of camomile, as breathing its scent was supposed to give the strength needed to overcome the disease.

Dry the flowers by tying them together in a bunch. Put a brown paper bag over the bunch, tie firmly and hang up until the flowers are dry. Don't put too many flowers in each bag.

Camomile Tea

Makes 1 jug   Preparation time: 5 minutes

1 teaspoon fresh or dried
*   camomile flowers per*
*   person*
Boiling water

1 Place the flowers in a large jug. Pour the boiling water over them.

2 Leave the flowers to infuse for 5 minutes. Sweeten the tea with a little sugar or honey as desired.

CENTAURY

Centaury grows in woodlands, fields and hedgerows and bears red flowers in July and August. The name comes from the myth that Chiron the centaur used the herb to heal Hercules of an arrow wound. It is supposed to stimulate the appetite and this is probably why it is a major ingredient of vermouth, a drink usually taken before meals. Adding a few leaves to home-made wine gives it a slightly vermouth-like flavour.

CHICKWEED

Chickweed survives all but the most bitter of weather so it is useful as a salad herb all year round. It is small and low growing with tiny, pointed bright green leaves. Chickweed can be found almost anywhere, especially on waste ground and rough lawns. As a child, I used to collect it for my budgie Peter who loved to have a clump in his cage.

Snip stems of chickweed with small, sharp scissors and wash the herb well before use. Combine it with crisply fried chopped bacon, a Cox's apple cut into cubes and some crunchy croûtons for a delicious salad. It can also be made into a spring soup.

Spring Soup

Serves 4   Preparation time: 10 minutes   Cooking time: 5 minutes

This makes a delicious starter at any time of the year.

575ml/1 pint chicken stock
6 spring onions, trimmed and
    chopped
1 large old potato, peeled and
    sliced
Large bowl of chickweed
4 tablespoons double cream
Croûtons
Salt and pepper

1 Place the stock in a large pan and bring it to the boil. Add the onions, potato and chickweed.

2 Simmer gently for 10 –15 minutes until the potato is just tender. Strain the liquid and push the vegetables through a blender. Stir the resulting purée into the hot stock. Season to taste.

Serving suggestion: Serve with a swirl of double cream and sprinkling of croûtons. The soup can be served either hot or cold.

COLTSFOOT

The brilliant yellow, daisy-like flowers of coltsfoot can be found on waste ground, on banks and in gravelly areas. The flowers appear in March before the leaves. Coltsfoot flowers were used in cough remedies and the root was dried and smoked like a tobacco as a cure for asthma. The flowers make a delicious light white wine.

Coltsfoot Wine

Makes 3 litres/6 pints   Storage: 2–3 months

The wine is made using only the petals of the flowers. The quickest way to remove them is using a small pair of sharp scissors.

4×1 litre/2 pint jugs of
  coltsfoot petals
1kg/2lb 3oz sugar
Juice of 2 lemons
Sachet of wine yeast

1 Put the petals into a large plastic bucket. Pour on 1.5litres/3 pints of boiling water. Leave to soak for 24 hours, stirring from time to time.

2 Strain the liquid through a muslin-lined sieve. Press the flowers to extract the maximum juice.

3 Add the lemon juice to the liquid. Start the yeast following the instructions on the packet.

4 Stir the sugar into 1.5 litres/3 pints of water and bring to the boil. Stir well until the sugar has dissolved.

5 Add the sugar solution to the liquid. Allow to cool to blood heat and then add the yeast. Cover and leave to ferment for 3 days.

6 Transfer to a fermentation jar fitted with an airlock. Make the quantity up to the top of the jar with cold boiled water.

7 Leave in a warm place until fermentation has stopped. Siphon the wine into a clean jar. Seal and leave for another month. Siphon again and bottle. The wine is ready to drink after 2–3 months' storage.

VIOLETS

The very first sweet violets appear in sheltered hedgerows towards the end of February. If February frosts have been particularly vicious then the violets may not appear until early April. Violets sometimes bloom in autumn – an event said to herald a great misfortune.

John Gerard, in his herbal of 1633, said:

'Violets have great prerogative above others, not only because the mind conceiveth a certain pleasure and recreation by smelling and handling these most odoriferous flowers, but also for that very many, by these violets, receive ornament and comely grace: for there be made of them garlands for the head, nosegays and posies, which are delightful to look on and pleasant to smell to.'

The name violet comes from the Latin form of the Greek name Ione. The legend goes that when Jupiter turned Io into a white heifer because he was afraid of Juno's jealousy, he made violets grow to provide food for her.

Crystallised Violets

Preparation time: 5–10 minutes plus overnight drying

Primroses can be crystallised in the same way.

Violet/primrose flowers (heads
   only)
Egg-white, beaten
3–4 drops rose-water
Caster sugar

1 Beat the rose-water into the egg-white. Gently paint the flowers with this mixture, using a soft brush.

2 Dip the flowers in caster sugar, shake them gently and leave overnight to dry.

Serving suggestion: Use to decorate cakes or small, fragrant ice-creams.

COWSLIP

Although cowslip wine was a great favourite when I was a child, these lovely yellow flowers are now far too rare to be picked. The moving of hedgerows, the development of monoculture (which means growing one kind of grass seed in place of former meadows) and the use of pesticides are largely to blame for their demise.

DANDELION

Known to generations of children as pissy beds, from the old Tudor name, piss-in-the-bed, dandelions have a marked diuretic effect. Their true name comes from the French dent-de-lion, literally 'like a lion's tooth'.

Dandelions are sometimes also known by the old country names Lion's Tooth, Priest's Crown and Puffball. Children for generations have blown the seeds from the fluffy seed-ladened puffball to tell the time, but even this activity has its darker side. It is said that if all the seeds are blown away, the child will be rejected by its mother. Another old tale claims that the number of puffs it took a young maid to blow all the seeds away showed the number of years she would have to wait for a husband.

Like most plants in British folklore, dandelions gathered on Midsummer Eve have magical properties to drive away the powers of mischief which are abroad on that night. Dandelions should be included in a midsummer garland to protect the house, byre and beasts. The garland should also include St John's Wort, Mugwort, Plantain, Corn Marigold, Dwarf Elder, Yarrow and Ivy. You can either hang the wreath on the door or burn it before nightfall.

Dandelion leaves are eaten as salad vegetable in France. They are delicious when young, but bitter and tough when old. Dandelion flowers make a very good, light wine.

Dandelion Wine

Makes 4 litres/1 gallon   Storage time: 6 months

This wine is made using the flowers of the dandelion. It tastes a little like Greek retsina, without tasting of disinfectant.

2×1 litre/2 pint jugs filled with
dandelion heads only
Wine-sterilising tablets
(optional)
1kg/2lb 3oz sugar
Sachet of wine yeast
1 teaspoon sugar
2 oranges
Half a lemon

1 Put the dandelion flowers into a large bucket and pour on 4 litres/1 gallon of boiling water. You can add wine-sterilising tablets at this point if you wish, but if the bucket is clean and sterilised this should not be necessary.

2 Cover the bucket and leave for 3 days, then strain the contents through a jelly-bag into another sterilised bucket. Pour the liquid into a demijohn.

3 Make a sugar syrup using the sugar and just enough water to dissolve it (approximately 425ml/¾pint). Heat the mixture gently, and when the sugar is at blood heat pour it into the demijohn with the dandelion liquid.

4 Mix the yeast with a little warmed water and 1 teaspoon of sugar. Leave in a warm place to ferment. Meanwhile add the grated rind and juice of the oranges and lemon to the demijohn.

5 When the yeast has started working, pour it into the demijohn. Seal this with an airlock and leave in a warm place until fermentation has stopped (when there are no more bubbles rising).

6 When fermentation has stopped siphon the wine into a clean jar. Fit an airlock and leave in a cool place until clear. Bottle and keep for 6 months before drinking.

Dandelion and Bacon Salad

Serves 4   Preparation and cooking time: 15 minutes

Tiny poached quail eggs and crunchy croûtons add a deliciously different touch to this salad.

Young dandelion leaves
Mixed lettuce leaves (oak leaf
   lettuce, curly endive, radiccio)
2 thick slices white bread
Oil
1 gammon steak
Vinaigrette
8 quail eggs

1 Wash the dandelion leaves and lettuce. Tear roughly and mix together in a large bowl.

2 Cut the bread into cubes. Heat the oil in a frying pan and fry the cubes of bread until golden brown. Drain on absorbent paper.

3 While the cubes of bread are cooking, grill the gammon steak.

4 Cut the gammon steak into cubes and keep in a warm place. Poach the quail eggs in boiling water.

5 Combine the salad ingredients, croûtons and gammon. Toss with vinaigrette. Spoon the quail eggs on to the top of the salad and serve immediately.

NETTLES

Nettles are the universal country medicine, and were especially used as a blood purifier. There is scientific evidence to prove that nettles lower both the blood sugar level and blood pressure. Although adult nettles have a vicious sting caused by formic acid which forms in the hairs on the leaves, young tender nettle shoots are harmless and are delicious in salads or gently steamed. Docks are, of course, the time-honoured remedy for nettle stings, hence the old rhyme, 'Nettle in dock out, Dock rub nettle out'.

The nettle grows almost everywhere. It is worth cultivating a patch in the garden to attract butterflies, as many caterpillars feed on the leaves. This in turn will attract birds, who feed on the caterpillars. Nettles were once cultivated to make cloth, as the stems contain fibres. A bunch of nettles thrown on the fire during a thunderstorm will protect the house from lightning. Dried nettles ward off flies and keep frogs away from beehives. The saying 'to grasp the nettle' springs from the belief that pulling up a nettle with bare hands would cure a fever. Aaron Hill wrote this 'nettle rhyme' in the eighteenth century:

'Tender handed stroke the nettle
And it stings you for your pains.
Grasp it like a man of mettle
And it soft as silk remains.'

A particularly nasty type of nettle, *Urtica pilulifera*, was introduced to Britain by the Romans. They flogged themselves with it to keep warm during the British winter. Roman nettles are now only found in Essex and on parts of the east coast.

Nettle Soup

Serves 4   Preparation time: 25 minutes   Cooking time: 35 minutes

Nettle soup is rather like spinach soup, but not as dark green and bitter.

575ml/1 pint jug young nettle
*   tops*
1 onion, chopped
1 large potato, peeled and diced
25g/1oz butter
575ml/1 pint chicken stock
150ml/¼ pint milk
150ml/¼ pint double cream
Pinch freshly grated nutmeg

1 Sauté the potato and onion in a pan with the butter until the onion is soft but not coloured.

2 Wash the nettles, and chop them finely (they can be chopped in a food processor). Add to the pan and stir to coat with the butter. Add the milk and chicken stock, and simmer for 25 minutes.

3 Purée this soup in a blender. Stir in the double cream and nutmeg and re-heat gently.

Serving suggestion: Serve with croûtons.

Nettle Beer

Makes 12 litres/2½ gallons

To make nettle beer equip yourself with scissors and a stout pair of gloves. The nettles must be picked when young. Nettle beer is a rather cloudy, greyish colour, rather like ginger beer, but delicious and light.

About 150 nettles, cut towards
the bottom of the stalk
1.5kg/3lb sugar
50g/2oz cream of tartar
15g/½oz yeast

1 Put the nettles into a large pan (a preserving pan is best) and boil with about 12 litres/2½ gallons of water. You may need to divide the nettles into batches if you haven't a pan large enough.

2 Strain the liquid from the nettles into another pan. Add the sugar and cream of tartar, stirring well. Heat and continue stirring until all the sugar has dissolved. Leave until tepid and then add the yeast.

3 Cover the pan and leave for 5 days. By then most of the fermentation will have stopped. Skim off the scum and siphon the liquid into another bucket. Siphoning prevents the sediment from being disturbed.

4 Bottle the beer using beer bottles with spring clips (Grolsch bottles are ideal). This will ensure the tops don't fly off.

Note: Nettle beer is best drunk within two to three months.

Nettle Pudding

Serves 4–6 Preparation time: 20 minutes Cooking time: 30–40 minutes

My grandmother used to make this pudding around Easter but she used pearl barley instead of rice. Rice gives a lighter result.

7×575ml/1 pint jugs full of
  young nettle tops
2 large onions, chopped
1 small spring cabbage
  (greyhound, primo or
  savoy)
75g/3oz half-cooked brown
  rice

1 Wash the nettle tops. Chop the cabbage. Mix the nettle tops, onions and cabbage.

2 Fill an oven-proof dish with alternating layers of this mixture and the rice. Cover and steam for 30 – 40 minutes until the vegetables are tender. Dot with butter and serve.

Serving suggestion: Nettle pudding goes well with roast meat.

WATERCRESS

When I was a child agricultural chemicals were virtually unknown, so wild watercress was always safe to eat (providing, of course, that it was picked from a stream not used by sheep or cattle, both of which can spread liver fluke). Today, widespread use of nitrates in agriculture, and other water pollution, means that only the remotest moorland watercress streams are really safe.

Watercress can be picked all summer. Pick the mature shoots with open leaves; do not pull the plant up by its roots. Wild watercress is much stronger in flavour than the cultivated type and has an astringent, peppery bite to it. Always wash it thoroughly in several changes of water. You will find a salad spinner useful for this.

Watercress is a wonderful source of iron, so is good for anyone who is anaemic. As a child I suffered badly from chilblains, and one of my great-aunts swore that by rubbing the affected toes with watercress the problem would be eased. Unfortunately it didn't work for me. Medieval herbalists used the plant for kidney disorders and other urinary infections, nervous illnesses and loss of appetite. It is also a very good source of vitamin C.

Watercress and Orange Salad

Serves 4   Preparation time: 15 minutes

This deliciously fresh salad is good with cold meats, especially poultry and game, or with hot duck.

Medium bunch wild
*   watercress*
2 oranges
1 medium onion
Vinaigrette

1 Wash the watercress and discard any tough stalks or yellowing leaves. Arrange the watercress in the bottom of a wide shallow dish.

2 Peel the oranges. Discard the pith and cut the oranges into slices. Arrange over the watercress.

3 Skin and slice the onion. Arrange onion rings over the oranges. Spoon a little vinaigrette over the salad and serve.

Watercress Soup

Serves 4   Preparation time: 20 minutes   Cooking time: 35 minutes

Wonderfully quick to make and just as good hot or cold. You can use half watercress, half lettuce if you wish.

Large bunch watercress
1 small onion, skinned and
   chopped
25g/1oz butter
300ml/½ pint chicken stock
150ml/¼ pint milk
150ml/¼ pint double cream
Croûtons or toasted almonds
   to serve

1 Wash the watercress and discard any yellowing leaves. Sauté in butter with the onion.

2 As soon as the watercress is limp, add the stock and milk. Simmer gently for 25 minutes.

3 Purée in a blender or processor. Stir in the double cream and re-heat gently.

Serving suggestion: Serve sprinkled with toasted almonds or croûtons.

PIGNUTS

Pignuts grow in meadowland and can be identified by a white, lacy flower which appears in June. Monoculture means that this plant is less common than it used to be. The great charm of the pignut lies in the tuberous root which is delicious either raw or cooked.

Cumbrian children called them 'yow yarlins', a name which may come from Old Norse. We used to dig up the tubers, wash them in the stream and eat them raw. My father could recall he and his friends boiling them in an old tin can of water as an accompaniment to baked trout, poached from the River Cocker.

Pignuts can be peeled and baked with meat like parsnips, boiled and served tossed with butter, or puréed.

TANSY

The yellow button-like flowers and feathery green leaves of tansy are common all over Britain. The flowers appear in July. The plant can be recognised by a camphoric smell given off when the leaves are rubbed. Tansy became the name for a sweet dish made from cream and eggs; the traditional time to eat one was at Easter, after the Lenten fast. Tansy was believed to cure worms thought to be caused by eating fish during Lent.

Sir Kenelm Digby, the Robert Carrier of his time, wrote the following recipe for an Easter tansy in 1669. It appeared in *The Closet of Sir Kenelm Digby Opened*:

'To make a tansy, take three pints of cream, fourteen New-laid eggs (the whites of seven put away), one pint of juice of Spinach, six or seven spoonfuls of juice of Tansy, a Nutmeg (or two) grated small, half a pound of sugar and a little salt. Beat all these well together, then fry it in a pan with no more Butter than is necessary. When it is enough, serve it up with juice of Orange or slices of Lemon upon it.'

The slightly spicy taste of tansy made it valuable as a substitute for real spices which only the rich could afford. Tansy was grown in most cottage gardens and used to flavour both sweet and savoury dishes. It actually tastes terrible — which could account for the enormous amounts of cream and sugar used in the making of tansies. People ate it believing that it would do them good. It was one of the strewing herbs, scattered over the floors of churches and law courts when plague was abroad. The leaves were also rubbed on meat in summer to keep the flies away.

BY THE SEA

As an island race the British have always made good use of the resources offered by the surrounding sea. The shoreline has as many riches as the sea, less well known than fish and shellfish, but just as good.

Our coastline varies from the great salt lands of East Anglia to the rocky drama of Scotland and the wide sands of the Solway. The plants that grow around the coast are just as diverse as those found inland. There are, however, a few rules to remember when collecting coastal plants:

- Stay away from any area where you might be cut off by the tide or might meet sinking sands. Always ask local advice.

- Several areas of the coast are used for military purposes. Keep out of restricted areas and off beaches marked with unexploded bomb or mine warnings.

- Don't collect plants from beaches around a nuclear power station or other industrial installation.

SAMPHIRE

Marsh samphire grows on tidal mud-flats mainly in eastern England, the South-West and Wales. The traditional day to pick samphire is the longest day of the year as the plant is supposed to taste better if washed by every tide. It tastes delicious and is sometimes called sea asparagus. Picking it can be risky, especially in areas where there is sinking mud. It can be bought, beautifully fresh, from the open market in Norwich.

Boiled Samphire

Serves 4   Preparation time: 15 minutes   Cooking time: 10 minutes

Wash the samphire well in several changes of water before use.

450g/1lb samphire
Salt
50g/2oz butter
Freshly ground black pepper

1 Tie the samphire in small bundles using cotton thread. Put these in a large pan of boiling, salted water, and boil for 10 minutes.

2 Lift them out of the water and undo the bundles. Melt the butter and pour over the samphire. Season with freshly ground black pepper. Eat off the stalk as you would asparagus.

Serving suggestion: Serve with fish.

SEA HOLLY

This is now a rare plant and should not be picked or dug up. It grows on sandy and shingly shores and has distinctive pale silvery green holly-like leaves. The root of sea holly used to be much sought after to make sweetmeats called eryngoes. Eryngoes are roots candied with rose-water and cinnamon. John Gerard gave the following eryngoe recipe in his herbal of 1633;

'The manner to condite Eryngoes. Refine sugar fit for the purpose and take a pound of it, the white of an egge and a pint of cleere water, boile them together and scum it, then let it boile until it be come to good strong syrup, and when it is boiled, as it cooleth add thereto a saucer full of Rose-water, a spoon full of Cinnamon water, and a graine of Muske, which had been infused together the night before, and now strained; into which syrup being more than halfe cold, put in your roots to soke and infuse until the next day; your roots being ordered in manner hereafter following.

These your roots being washed and picked, must be boiled in faire water by the space of four houres, until they be soft then must they be pilled cleane as ye pill parsneps, and the pith must be drawne out at the end of the root; and if there be any whose pith cannot be drawne out at the end, then you must split them and so take out the pith; these you must also keep from much handling that they may be cleane, let them remaine in the syrup till the next day, and then set them on the fire in a faire broad pan until they be verie hot, but let them not boile at all; let them there remaine over the fire an houre or more, removing them easily in the pan from one place to another with a wooden slice. This done, have in redinesse great cap or royall papers, whereupon you must strew some sugar, upon which lay your roots after that you have taken them out of the pan. These papers you must put into a stove, or hot house to harden, but if you have not such a place, lay them before a good fire. In this manner if you condite your roots, there are not any that can prescribe you a better way. And thus may you condite any other root whatsoever, which will not only bee exceeding delicate but very wholesome, and effectual against diseases'.

LAVER

Laver is a type of seaweed which grows on rocks and stones. It can be found on the majority of coasts but is most famous in Wales. It grows in large, thin, dark sheets and is easy to collect. Laver is high in protein and vitamins. Laver bread is one of the national dishes of Wales; however, this is not an actual bread but a thick green purée. In some areas of Wales the purée is spread on fried bread and served with bacon. The more traditional use is to make it into oat cakes.

Laver Bread

Makes approximately ½lb   Preparation time: 20 minutes   Cooking time: 1–1½ hours

This keeps in the refrigerator for about a week.

2 large jugs of laver

1 Wash the laver thoroughly in several changes of water. Make sure you get rid of all the sand.

2 Lay the sheets of laver in a steamer. Steam for 1–1½ hours until the sheets have broken into little pieces. Purée. Drain away excess liquid and store the laver in the refrigerator.

SEA PURSLANE

Sea purslane grows in great patches on salt marshes below the high tide mark. It flourishes in thick, sticky mud, so do be careful when collecting it. It has small, oval, green leaves and must be washed in several changes of water before it can be used. It is good cooked without water in the same way as spinach. Toss with butter to serve. Pickled purslane can be bought in some areas of France. You can pickle your own purslane by blanching, packing into jars and covering with white wine vinegar.

FENNEL

Fennel grows wild on roadsides near the sea, on cliffs and on sand dunes. The road to Southwold harbour in Suffolk is lined with it, and the air is rich with the smell of aniseed on summer evenings. Local restaurants there pick it to serve with fish. I often use it in salads or braised like celery. If you are barbecuing fish, add a few sticks of fennel to the charcoal. It imparts a wonderful flavour, especially to oily fish such as mackerel.

The Romans brought cultivated fennel to Britain. They valued both the stalks and the seeds, and believed that the plant promoted bravery in soldiers. In medieval times it was used against witchcraft and the powers of darkness. Wild fennel is not the same plant as the bulb you buy in supermarkets, and the root of the wild fennel is rather bitter.

Braised Fennel

Serves 4   Preparation time: 10 minutes   Cooking time: 30 minutes

8 fennel stalks cut into short
   lengths
50g/2 oz butter
Freshly ground black pepper

1 Put the fennel into a heavy-based pan with the butter. Add a little water.

2 Cover with a layer of foil and a lid. Cook over a low heat for 30 minutes, or until the fennel is tender. Shake the pan occasionally.

Serving suggestion: Serve as a vegetable with fish or meat.

SEA BEET

Sea beet has big, glossy, dark green leaves and is the ancestor of most cultivated beets. The difference is that the root of the sea beet has no use as a food; it is the leaves which can be eaten. Sea beet grows on seashores in England and Wales but is little known in Scotland. The leaves can be picked from May until the first frosts of December and cooked in the same way as spinach.

26

CHAPTER 2

FUNGI AND MUSHROOMS

Although we have 390 native mushrooms and other fungi in Britain, many of them edible, we don't really take advantage of their bounty. One of the major reasons for this is that some fungi are deadly poisonous, whilst others can make you unpleasantly ill, and in many cases it is difficult to spot the difference between the safe and the dangerous. For this reason, only those fungi which cannot be mistaken for anything else have been included – also because they taste good enough to be well worth picking. It is wise in any case to equip yourself with a good full-colour guide to fungi before you go mushrooming. It is very important to avoid any fungus or mushroom about which you are unsure.

MOREL

Morel is the most delicious of our native fungi, and the most sought-after. The fungus appears from March to May, normally in sandy, chalky districts. It is an ochre yellow colour and looks like a honeycomb. There are several different species of morel. The best for eating is *Morchella rotunda* which can usually be found beneath broad-leaf trees. Always cut morels in half and wash carefully before use, as wood-lice, earwigs and other creatures can lurk inside the honeycomb-like cavities. Morel is very good dried. To dry it properly cut the fungus in half and wash it carefully. Pat the pieces dry with paper towels and then thread them on to a fine string, using a darning needle. Hang them up in a warm place to dry thoroughly. When they are dry, store them in an airtight jar. To use, soak in water for 30 minutes, or use in casseroles and sauces with pasta in their dried state.

Creamy Morel Flan

Serves 4 as a main course, 8 as a starter   Preparation time: 40 minutes   Cooking time: 20–25 minutes

This is a treat to serve on very special occasions, preferably in the morel season.

For the pastry:
50g/2oz butter
100g/4oz plain flour
Pinch of salt
1 egg

For the filling:
450g/1lb morels
25g/1oz butter
1 tablespoon plain flour
1 tablespoon dry sherry
275ml/½ pint double cream
Salt
Freshly ground black pepper

1 Cut the butter into small cubes. Sift the flour and salt into a bowl and rub the butter in until the mixture resembles fine breadcrumbs.

2 Beat the egg and add gradually to the pastry to form a smooth dough. Wrap the dough in clingfilm and chill for 30 minutes.

3 While the dough is chilling, heat the oven to 200°C/400°F/Gas Mark 6. Slice and wash the morels. When the pastry is ready, use it to line a 20cm/8in flan tin. Bake blind for 10 minutes.

4 Meanwhile sauté the mushrooms in the butter. Stir in the flour and cook for a further 1 minute. Gradually stir in the sherry and the cream. Cook very gently until it has thickened, then season to taste.

5 Pour the filling into the flan case. Bake for 10–12 minutes.

Serving suggestion: Serve hot or cold.

Morels on a Croûte

Serves 1   Preparation time: 10 minutes   Cooking time: 25 minutes

This is a sophisticated version of mushrooms on toast, the traditional English savoury. Savouries were served after or instead of dessert right up until the 1950s. Sadly the savoury has now disappeared from many hotel and restaurant menus. The quantities given here are for one person only. If you wish to serve more simply multiply the quantities.

2 morels
15g/½oz butter
1 slice white bread
Olive oil
2 tablespoons double cream
Freshly chopped parsley

Pre-heat the oven to 200°C/400°F/Gas Mark 6

1 Wash and slice the morels. Sauté in the butter for 15 minutes. Stir in just enough plain flour to bind the mixture together. Cook for a further 30 seconds and then stir in the cream. Cook for another 1 minute and then remove from the heat.

2 Cut the crusts off the bread. Dip the slice in olive oil, making sure that both sides are coated. Place the bread on the oven shelf and bake for 10 minutes or until golden and crunchy.

Serving suggestion: The morel mixture is served on the croûte and garnished with freshly chopped parsley.

ST GEORGE'S MUSHROOM

St George's mushroom is so called because it is supposed to appear on St George's Day (23 April), although its appearance in late June is more common. This mushroom grows in woodland, on pasture and sometimes on roadsides, usually in small groups or in rings. It is creamy-white, beige or pinkish in colour with cream-coloured gills on the underside. It can be as large as 15cm/6in across the cap.

St George's mushroom is excellent fried in butter and served with bacon and eggs, made into soup, in casseroles or for mushroom sauce. It can be dried but does lose some of its flavour.

St George's Omelette

Serves 2   Preparation time: 10 minutes   Cooking time: 10 minutes

Omelettes must be freshly cooked to taste really good. Two is the maximum number it is sensible to cook omelettes for, as they can then be eaten almost straight from the pan.

225g/8oz St George's
  mushrooms
50g/2oz butter
6 eggs
Salt
Freshly ground black pepper

1 Wash and wipe the mushrooms. Slice the caps from the stalks. (The stalks can be saved to use in a casserole or in a soup.) Sauté the mushroom caps in half the butter. Set aside.

2 Lightly beat the eggs with a little water and seasoning. Put the remaining butter in a hot omelette pan. As soon as the butter starts to sizzle pour in half of the egg mixture. Swirl it around with a fork. When the egg begins to set around the edges, lift it gently so that the remaining liquid runs beneath.

3 When the omelette is just firm, but not set in the centre, spoon half of the mushrooms over one half of the omelette and flip the other half over the top to form a parcel, with the mushrooms inside. Remove from the pan and keep warm. Cook the other omelette in the same way.

Serving suggestion: Serve as a delicious breakfast, or as a snack.

St George's Risotto

Serves 4   Preparation time: 10 minutes   Cooking time: 25–30 minutes

The robust flavour of St George's mushrooms makes them a good choice to combine with rice. You can also add chicken, ham or other leftovers of cooked meat for a little extra taste.

75g/3oz butter
1 onion, skinned and chopped
450g/1lb St George's
  mushrooms, sliced
450g/1lb long grain easy-cook
  rice
575ml/1 pint chicken stock
4 hard-boiled eggs
Freshly chopped parsley

1 Melt the butter in a large saucepan. Sauté the onions for 3–4 minutes, then add the mushrooms. Cook for 5 minutes. Stir in the rice and cook, stirring until the rice looks translucent. Add the stock, ensuring that there is just enough liquid to cover the rice.

2 Simmer gently until all the stock has been absorbed and the rice is tender.

Serving suggestion: Turn into a heated dish. Arrange sliced hard-boiled eggs and chopped parsley on the top.

JEW'S EAR

This is a tree fungus which is found when the weather is warm, wet and humid. It grows on elder trees and it is thought that the name is a corruption of Judas' Ear, as Judas Iscariot hanged himself on an elder, hence the elder's sinister reputation (*see* elderberries, page 68). The fungus is ear-shaped and reddish-brown in colour. It is edible, if not particularly tasty, but it does contain some medicinal properties, as Pechy explained in his herbal, published in 1694:

'It grows to the Trunk of the Elder-Tree. Being dried, it will keep a good Year. Boyl'd in milk or infus'd in Vinegar, 'tis good to gargle the mouth or throat in Quinsies and other inflammations of the Mouth and Throat and being infus'd in some proper Water, it is good in diseases of the Eyes.'

CHANTERELLES

Chanterelles (sometimes called girolles) are the aristocrats among wild mushrooms. They are very popular in Europe and served almost as we serve the ubiquitous cultivated mushroom. Here you may be lucky enough to find some golden yellow chanterelles in woodland. They usually grow beneath pine, beech or birch trees. They are easy to recognise, not only because of their distinctive colour, but also by the cup shape and the gills which run down the stem. An apricoty smell is another good way to recognise them.

Chanterelles are delicious fried in butter with a little chopped onion, garlic and some parsley. They have a natural affinity to eggs. Sauté some in butter and stir into scrambled eggs for a luxury breakfast, or serve on slices of hot, buttered toast.

Hunter's Mushrooms

Serves 4   Preparation time: 15 minutes   Cooking time: 25 minutes

If you can find enough chanterelles this is a deliciously filling dish.

1kg/2lb 3oz chanterelles
100g/4oz butter
8 rashers bacon, de-rinded
  and cut into strips
450g/1lb new potatoes,
  scrubbed but not scraped
150ml/¼pint double cream
Freshly ground black pepper
Freshly chopped parsley

1 Wash the chanterelles and trim the ends of the stems. Sauté them in 25g/1oz butter. Lift out with a slotted spoon and set aside.

2 Fry the bacon strips in the remaining butter until just brown. Reduce heat, add the mushrooms and leave to simmer for 15 minutes.

3 In the meantime, cook the new potatoes in boiling, salted water until just tender. Cut the potatoes into chunks. Add to the mushrooms and toss the contents of the pan together so that the potatoes become coated with mushroom juice. Stir in the cream and cook over a low heat for 1 minute.

Serving suggestion: Sprinkle with freshly chopped parsley, season to taste with black pepper and serve.

SHAGGY INK CAP

This mushroom grows almost everywhere, and is long and thin with a scaly cap. It is also sometimes called Lawyer's Wig, Shaggy Cap or Shaggy Mane. It goes black very quickly and when cooked gives off large quantities of juice. The Shaggy Ink Cap is good with fish dishes, fried in butter and served on a croûte, gently stewed with cream, or added to almost any dish which requires mushroom.

Mushroom and Potato Gratin

Serves 4   Preparation time: 10 minutes   Cooking time: 30 minutes

The distinctive flavour of the Ink Cap blends well with the blandness of potato. Add a little bacon, cut into strips and sautéd.

450g/1lb Ink Caps
25g/1oz butter
25g/1oz plain flour
275ml/½ pint milk
150ml/¼ pint double cream
Salt
Freshly ground black pepper
350g/12oz mashed potatoes

Pre-heat the oven to 200°C/400°F/Gas Mark 6

1 Wipe the mushrooms. Slice the caps off and discard the stems. Sauté the mushrooms in the butter for 4–5 minutes.

2 Stir the flour into the mushrooms. Cook for 1 minute, then gradually stir in the milk and cream. Stir gently over low heat until thickened.

3 Season to taste. Butter an ovenproof dish, put half the mashed potato in the bottom and pour on the mushrooms. Cover with the remainder of the potato. Bake for 15–20 minutes until the top is browned.

Serving suggestion: Serve hot.

BEEFSTEAK

Large, fleshy-looking and ochre yellow, the beefsteak is a common sight in autumn. It grows on the trunk of oak and chestnut trees, so it is usually found in broad-leaved woodlands. Beefsteak becomes woody when it is old, so break a small piece off before you pick the fungus to check the condition of the flesh.

To use beefsteak, wash it carefully and cut it into slices. The inside looks like meat, hence the name. The nicest way to serve it is sautéd in butter with some chopped shallots, garlic, herbs and a glass of white wine. Cook for 10–15 minutes until the liquid has reduced.

PARASOL MUSHROOM

These leggy, beige-brown mushrooms are common in woodlands and fields from July to November. The cap is parasol-shaped and scaly. Parasol mushrooms are tender and delicate, so should be cooked quickly. They are good lightly sautéd to add to scrambled eggs or an omelette, but lose flavour if used in a casserole or other dish which needs prolonged cooking.

PUFF-BALLS

I was brought up to believe that all puff-balls were deadly poisonous. They are thought to be very unlucky in some parts of Britain and children were encouraged to squash them wherever they appeared. All

British puff-balls are safe to eat, but are only worth using when they are white all the way through. They can vary in size from that of a walnut to bigger than a football. Dried puff-balls were once used as fire-lighters.

Puff-balls can be found growing on pasture, lawns and near hedges. To cook, wipe the puff-balls and cut into slices of 5mm/¼in thick. Puff-balls can be fried with bacon for breakfast, sautéd in butter and served on toast. Alternatively put them beneath the joint for the last 30 minutes of cooking, batter and deep fry to serve with tartare sauce, or simply add to casseroles.

CEPS

The cep is sometimes called edible boletus. It is a common sight in coniferous and broad-leaved woodlands but has a particular affinity for beech trees. The cap is brownish-gold in colour, sometimes slightly shiny, and the mushroom stands about 15cm/6in high, and about the same across the cap. It has a nutty flavour and is regarded as a great delicacy in France and Italy where you will find many dishes containing ceps.

Ceps can be used in any dish requiring mushrooms, but don't eat them raw as they can cause a stomach upset. They are best sautéd, fried in breadcrumbs or batter, and used in stuffings. Ceps can be dried, as described for morels (*see* page 27) and added to casseroles, soups and stews.

Cep Soup

Serves 4   Preparation time: 5 minutes   Cooking time: 30 minutes

The lovely flavour of the cep means that no stock is needed for this soup.

450g/1lb ceps (caps only)
75g/3oz butter
275ml/½ pint milk
275ml/½ pint double cream
Freshly ground black pepper
Freshly chopped parsley

1 Roughly chop the ceps. Sauté in butter for 15 minutes. Add the milk and cream.

2 Simmer gently for 15 minutes. Purée in a blender, then re-heat gently.

Serving suggestion: Serve sprinkled with chopped parsley and crunchy croûtons.

Cep Sauce for Pasta

Serves 4   Preparation time: 10 minutes   Cooking time: 15 minutes

Cultivated mushrooms are sometimes rather too mild to make a really good sauce for pasta, but the nutty flavour of the cep is perfect. This recipe gives sufficient sauce for a pasta dish for four people.

450g/1lb ceps (caps only)
1 small onion, finely chopped
1 garlic clove, skinned and
  crushed
50g/2oz butter
50g/2oz pine nuts
Freshly chopped parsley
Grated Parmesan

1 Wipe the ceps. Slice and set aside.

2 Sauté the onion and garlic in the butter for 4 minutes or so until soft. Add the ceps and cook for 10 minutes.

3 Add the parsley and the pine nuts towards the end of cooking time. While the mushrooms are cooking, prepare the pasta in the usual way. Toss the pasta with Parmesan and a little butter. Gently stir in the sauce and serve.

Serving suggestion: This sauce can be served with either tagliatelle or spaghetti.

FIELD MUSHROOMS

There is nothing quite so delicious as a large, fresh, field mushroom fried in butter and served with bacon and eggs. Sadly, agricultural progress, particularly monoculture (where meadows are sown with just one type of grass rather than the natural mixture of flowers, grasses and mushrooms), has seen the decline of the field mushroom. My father loved mushrooming and would rise at dawn in summer and early autumn, wake the dog (who would rather have stayed in bed), and trek the fields behind our house in search of breakfast.

The field mushroom is the ancestor of the cultivated fungus we buy in the shops, but a totally different creature in terms of flavour. The mushrooms grow in small groups or singly and can be tiny and button-shaped or open and as large as a dinner plate. When the mushrooms are fresh, the gills are pale pink. These turn darker as the fungus ages.

Field mushrooms can be used in any recipe which calls for mushrooms. They are wonderful simply grilled and served on toast. A big, meaty field mushroom, grilled with butter and served with French bread to mop up the juice, is a meal in itself.

Garlic Mushrooms

Serves 2 as a main course, or 4 as a starter   Preparation time: 15 minutes   Cooking time: 30–40 minutes

As the mushrooms cook they give out a delicious juice which combines wonderfully with the butter and garlic.

700g/1½lb field mushrooms
225g/8oz butter, softened
2 plump garlic cloves, skinned
 and crushed
3 tablespoons lemon juice
Freshly chopped parsley

Pre-heat the oven to 150°C/300°F/Gas Mark 2

1 Remove the stalks from the mushrooms. They can be used for stock or in a casserole.

2 Wipe the mushroom caps. Cream together the crushed garlic, butter, lemon juice and parsley.

3 Divide the butter mixture between the mushrooms, spreading it into the caps. Put the mushrooms in a single layer in a large dish. Cover with foil. ·

4 Bake for 30–40 minutes, until the butter has melted and the mushrooms have given up their juice.

Serving suggestion: Serve with lots of crusty bread.

Mushroom Purée

Serves 4   Preparation time: 20 minutes   Cooking time: 30 minutes

Mushroom purée is delicious as a starter or as an anytime snack. The quantities given should be sufficient for four servings.

400g/14oz field mushrooms
100g/4oz butter
Salt
Freshly ground black pepper

1 Wipe the mushrooms and chop them roughly. Melt the butter in a heavy-based saucepan over a medium heat.

2 Add the mushrooms to the butter and cover. Cook over a low heat for 30 minutes until dark and juicy.

3 Purée the mushrooms with their juice in a blender. Season to taste.

Serving suggestion: Mushroom purée can be served spread on to slices of crisp toast and topped with a poached egg.

Mushroom Sauce

Serves 4   Preparation time: 10 minutes   Cooking time: 15 minutes

This sauce is delicious served with fish, chicken or other white meats. It can also be used as the basis for a pie filling. Simply add chunks of cooked chicken, ham or raw white fish.

225g/8oz field mushrooms
50g/2oz butter
25g/1oz plain flour
275ml/½ pint milk
4 tablespoons double cream
Salt
Freshly ground black pepper
Freshly chopped parsley

1 Wipe and chop the mushrooms. Melt the butter in a heavy-based pan. Add the mushrooms and sauté them for 3 − 4 minutes.

2 Stir in the flour and cook for 1 minute. Gradually stir in the milk, and keep stirring slowly until thickened.

3 Stir in the cream. Season to taste and stir in the parsley.

CHAPTER 3

NUTS

Although Britain can boast only a few native nuts they are all delicious and are well worth the effort of finding and picking. The nutting season traditionally began on 14 September, known as Holy Cross or Holy Rood Day, and sometimes known as the Holy Nut Day or Devil's Nutting Day. Nuts were a valuable food source for the winter and greatly prized.

When gathering nuts take a stout walking stick with you to pull the branches down. Pick the nuts carefully and do not damage the tree.

HAZEL

Hazel or cob nuts can be found on bushy trees in hedges, coppices and on rough ground. Until World War II many country schools closed on 14 September, the day regarded to be the most propitious time to pick hazels. Hazels picked on Holy Rood Day have magical properties, and a double nut will ward off rheumatism, toothache or witchcraft!

The hazel plays an important part in Celtic literature and is surrounded by superstition. It is unlucky to pick nuts on a Sunday, for the Devil then lives in the hazel. Gathering unripe nuts is also considered unlucky. Markham's *English Husbandman* of 1635 says:

'For nuts you shall know they are ripe as soon as you perceive them a little brown within the husk, or as it were, ready to fall out of the same. After they be gathered, you shall shale them and take them clean out of their husks; then for preserving them from either worms or dryness, it shall be good to lay them in some low cellar, where you cover them with sand, being first put into great bags or bladders.'

Nuts were not always a good thing – as a September 1794 edition of the *York Courant* warned:

'As a caution to persons at this season when nuts are so very abundant, we state that the sudden death of Mr Nunn of Cley, Norfolk, is generally attributed to eating a great quantity of filberts and drinking port wine therewith.'

As a child I picked nuts with my friend Liz, and my grandmother made these into wonderful nut toffee.

Nut Taffy

Makes 225g/½lb Preparation time: 10 minutes Cooking time: 5 minutes

This is the toffee my grandmother made. It tastes as good today as it did in my childhood and makes a lovely present if packed in a pretty tin.

225g/8oz hazelnuts
100g/4oz butter
225g/8oz granulated sugar
2 tablespoons malt vinegar
2 tablespoons golden syrup

1 Place the hazelnuts under a hot grill for a couple of minutes, then rub away the skins. Grease 2 shallow toffee tins.

2 Put the butter into a heavy pan and melt it over a low heat. Stir in the sugar, vinegar and syrup. Keep stirring until the sugar has melted.

3 Bring to the boil and boil for about 5 minutes, stirring from time to time. When the mixture turns golden, test by dropping a little into cold water. If the toffee turns brittle it is ready. If not, continue boiling.

4 As soon as the toffee is ready stir the nuts in then pour the mixture on to the trays. When the toffee is half set mark it into squares with a sharp knife. When it is fully set you can break it into the squares to eat.

Panforte

Makes 450g/1lb   Preparation time: 25 minutes   Cooking time: 30 minutes

This traditional Italian nougat is rich and delicious, and perfect served with drinks.

75g/3oz hazelnuts
75g/3oz almonds
75g/3oz candied orange peel
75g/3oz candied lemon peel
50g/2oz plain flour
25g/1oz plain flour
25g/1oz cocoa powder
1½ teaspoons ground
   cinnamon
100g/4oz honey
100g/4oz caster sugar
A little icing sugar, sifted

Pre-heat the oven to 160°C/350°F/Gas Mark 3

1 Grease the base and sides of a 20cm/8in cake tin with a removable base. Line the tin with non-stick silicone paper.

2 Lightly toast the nuts under a hot grill, then rub the skins away.

3 Chop all the peel and put it into a bowl. Stir in the nuts, flour, cocoa powder and spices. Mix well.

4 Put the honey and sugar into a pan with a teaspoon of water. Heat gently, stirring until the sugar melts, then bring the mixture to the boil until it reaches 125°C/240°F on a sugar thermometer.

5 Stir in the dry ingredients, pour the mixture into the prepared cake tin and spread flat. Bake for 30 minutes, then turn out of the tin, peel away the paper and dust with icing sugar. Cut into slivers to serve.

Serving suggestion: Serve as a snack or teatime treat.

Hazelnut Fudge

Makes 450g/1lb   Preparation time: 1 hour   Cooking time: 15 minutes

Sinfully delicious, and another lovely gift for a sweet-toothed friend.

150ml/¼ pint milk
550g/1¼lb granulated sugar
50g/2oz butter
225g/8oz hazelnuts, chopped

1 Put the milk and sugar into a large pan and leave aside for 45 minutes. Grease two toffee tins. Add the butter to the sugar and milk and heat slowly, stirring until the sugar has dissolved.

2 Bring the mixture to the boil and simmer for 15 minutes, stirring from time to time. Drop some of the mixture into a cup of cold water. If it forms a soft ball it is ready.

3 Stir in the chopped hazelnuts then pour the mixture into the prepared tins. Mark into squares when half set; these can be broken up when the fudge is fully set.

Spiced Hazelnuts

Makes 450g/1lb   Preparation time: 10 minutes   Cooking time: 15 minutes

An unusual change from the traditional peanuts, to be served with drinks. Keep the nuts in an airtight tin.

450g/1lb hazelnuts
2 tablespoons cooking oil
2 tablespoons curry powder
1 teaspoon soy sauce
1 teaspoon Worcestershire sauce
Pinch of garlic powder
Salt
Freshly ground black pepper

Pre-heat the oven to 200°C/400°F/Gas Mark 6

1 Put the nuts under a hot grill for 2 minutes and then rub away the outer skins. Heat the oil in the frying pan.

2 Stir in the spices and sauces. Stir in the nuts and cook for 2 minutes.

3 Put the nuts into a shallow dish and bake for 15 minutes, then drain on paper towels.

Serving suggestion: Sprinkle with a little salt to serve.

Hazelnut Meringue Cake

Makes 1 cake   Preparation time: 30 minutes   Cooking time: 45 minutes

Raspberries are the best topping for this mouthwatering dessert. As the nuts and raspberries are not in season at the same time, use frozen fruit.

6 egg-whites
350g/12oz caster sugar
150g/5oz ground hazelnuts
275ml/½ pint double cream
Raspberries
Icing sugar

Pre-heat the oven to 170°C/325°F/Gas Mark 3

1 Whisk the egg-whites until they are stiff. Whisk in half the sugar until the mixture is stiff and glossy, then fold the other half of the sugar in. Stir in the ground hazelnuts.

2 Grease three 25cm/9in loose-bottomed cake tins and line with non-stick silicone paper. Pour in the mixture, dividing equally between the tins.

3 Bake the meringues for 45 minutes. Remove from the oven, allow to cool slightly, then remove from the tins and peel away the paper. Leave to cool on wire trays.

4 Whip the cream and sandwich the meringues together with fruit and cream.

Serving suggestion: Top with frozen raspberries or any other fruit and sprinkle with icing sugar before serving.

SWEET CHESTNUTS

The sweet chestnut was originally brought to Britain by the Romans. It is now largely neglected, other than for making chestnut stuffing and serving with Brussels sprouts. However, in Europe sweet chestnuts are made into a wide variety of sweet and savoury dishes. My father used to collect chestnuts from Sand Lane in Cockermouth and roast them on a shovel in the fireplace. London still has hot-chestnut men who appear on the streets in September and October.

Horse chestnuts (conkers) and sweet chestnuts are easily differentiated. The horse chestnut has a hard, spiky green husk whilst the husk of the sweet chestnut is covered in softer hairy green-brown spines.

Brussels Sprouts with Chestnuts

Serves 6   Preparation time: 1 hour   Cooking time: 40 minutes

This is the traditional accompaniment to Christmas lunch.

350g/12oz chestnuts
275ml/½ pint chicken stock
1 celery stick
Pinch of soft brown sugar
700g/1½lb Brussels sprouts,
   trimmed
Salt
Knob of butter

1 Cut a cross in the base of each chestnut. Put the nuts in cold water. Bring to the boil and leave until the water is cold, then peel away the skins using a sharp knife.

2 Cut the celery into short lengths. Place it into a pan with the skinned chestnuts, sugar and stock. Simmer for 40 minutes.

3 While the nuts are cooking, cook the sprouts in boiling salted water for 10 minutes. Drain.

4 When cooked, lift the nuts out with a slotted spoon and mix with the drained sprouts. Toss with a knob of butter.

Serving suggestion: Serve hot.

Marrons Glacés

Makes 12 oz   Standing time: 36 hours   Cooking time: 30 minutes

It is difficult to make authentic marrons glacés under home conditions but these taste delicious and are almost the same as the expensive, commercially produced variety.

225g/8oz granulated sugar
225g/8oz glucose (available
  from chemists)
350g/12oz whole chestnuts,
  peeled
Vanilla essence

1 Put the sugar and the glucose into a large heavy-based pan with 175ml/6fl oz cold water. Bring to the boil, stirring.

2 Add the chestnuts and bring to the boil again. Remove from the heat and leave overnight in a warm place.

3 Bring the chestnuts and syrup to the boil again, then leave overnight once more.

4 Add 6–8 drops of vanilla essence and boil again. Lift the chestnuts out of the syrup and put them in warmed, sterilised bottling jars.

5 Pour the syrup over the chestnuts. Test that the jars have sealed properly – the lid should stay on when you release the spring clip.

Serving suggestion: Serve with ice-cream as a luxury dessert.

Chestnut Stuffing

Makes sufficient to stuff a 5.5kg/12lb bird   Preparation time: 15 minutes   Cooking time: 30 minutes

The traditional Christmas alternative to sage and onion stuffing. Stuff the neck cavity of the bird so that the stuffing can be served cut into slices. Skin the chestnuts first then simmer them in stock for 20 minutes before chopping.

450g/1lb chestnuts, skinned
   and chopped
25g/1oz butter
2 medium onions, skinned and
   chopped
350g/12oz fresh breadcrumbs
75g/3oz shredded suet or
   chopped bacon
3 tablespoons horseradish
Lemon juice
Salt
Freshly ground black pepper

1 Melt the butter in a frying pan and stir in the onions. Cook until soft.

2 Add the chestnuts and other ingredients. Cook for 10 minutes then take off the heat and cool.

3 Spoon the stuffing into the neck cavity of the bird, then roast it in the usual way.

WALNUTS

Although walnut trees were mostly grown on great estates you may find the odd specimen which has seeded and is flourishing in the wild. The tree is a native of the Balkans and was probably brought to Britain in the fifteenth century. There is a curious country belief that beating the trunk of a mature walnut gives a fruitful harvest:

   'A woman, a witch and a walnut tree
   The more you beat them, the better they be.'

As well as being prized for its wood, which is used in the manufacture of fine furniture, the walnut produces delicious nuts. A mature walnut tree can yield up to 150lb of nuts, which are picked in July when they are green or 'wet' for pickling, and in October when ripe for storage in airtight containers during the winter months.

Use the kernels of the ripe nut in baking, for stuffings, tossed with salad, in breads and cakes or mixed with celery, chopped apple and mayonnaise.

Pickled Walnuts

Makes 1kg/2lb 3oz   Preparation time: 5 days   Cooking time: 10 minutes   Storage time: 2 months

The shells of the nuts turn crumbly in the pickling vinegar. Serve pickled walnuts with cold meats and raised pie.

1kg/2lb 3oz green walnuts
A handful of pickling spice
    (mixture of black and white
    peppercorns, mace, cloves,
    cinnamon, bruised ginger
    root and coriander)
Salt
Malt vinegar

1 Prick the walnut shells with a darning needle. Put them into a large plastic bucket and cover with brine, made using 225g/8oz salt to every gallon of cold water.

2 Leave the nuts in the brine for 5 days. Lift them out and leave to dry, preferably in the sun.

3 The walnuts will turn black during drying. Once dry, pack the nuts into jars. Put the pickling spice into a pan with enough vinegar to cover the nuts. Bring the vinegar to the boil, then leave to cool. When cold, pour over the nuts. They are ready to eat in about 2 months. The nuts keep as long as they are covered by vinegar.

Walnut Ketchup

Preparation and cooking time: 45 minutes   Storage time: 1 year

Walnut ketchup was popular in the eighteenth and nineteenth centuries and was served with meats; it tastes rather like Worcestershire sauce. The ketchup takes over a year to mature.

450g/1lb green walnuts
Enough vinegar to cover the
    walnuts
225g/8oz anchovies
2 plump garlic cloves
1 tablespoon whole mace
1 tablespoon black pepper
1 tablespoon ground ginger

1 Prick the walnut shells with a darning needle. Put them into a large jar and cover with vinegar. Seal the jar and keep for 1 year in a dark place.

2 Strain the liquid. Pound the anchovies and whole spices. Stir into the walnut vinegar with the ginger.

3 Bring to the boil and simmer until reduced by half, then bottle. The walnuts can be used as pickled walnuts, but they won't be very spicy.

Walnut Tart

Serves 6   Preparation and chilling time: 50 minutes   Cooking time: 45 minutes

An English version of American pecan pie.

50g/2oz plain flour
50g/2oz butter
15g/¹/₂oz caster sugar
15g/¹/₂oz ground almonds
3 eggs
225g/8oz golden syrup
50g/2oz caster sugar
100g/4oz shelled walnuts
Vanilla essence

Pre-heat the oven to 180°C/350°F/Gas Mark 4

1 Grease a 20cm/8in loose-bottomed flan tin.

2 Sift the flour into a bowl. Cut the butter into small cubes and rub into the flour. Stir in the ground almonds and sugar, then add enough water to form a firm dough.

3 Chill the dough for 30 minutes, then roll out to line the flan tin.

4 Beat the eggs then stir in all the other ingredients and add vanilla essence to taste – 2 or 3 drops is usually enough. Pour the mixture into the flan case.

5 Bake for 45 minutes.

Serving suggestion: Serve cold with whipped cream.

Cheese and Walnut Bread

Makes 350g/12oz loaf   Preparation time: 25 minutes   Cooking time: 1 hour

This is best eaten when really fresh as, like all non-yeast breads, it stales quickly.

225g/8oz self-raising flour
1 teaspoon English mustard
*   powder*
1 teaspoon salt
Freshly ground black pepper
75g/3oz butter
100g/4oz mature Cheddar
*   cheese, grated*
50g/2oz walnuts, chopped
2 eggs
Milk to mix

Pre-heat the oven to 180°C/350°F/Gas Mark 4

1 Sieve the flour, mustard and salt into a bowl. Add a grinding of pepper.

2 Cut the butter into cubes and rub into the flour until the mixture resembles fine breadcrumbs.

3 Stir in the cheese and walnuts. Beat the eggs with about 150ml/¼ pint milk (you may need more) and mix with the dry ingredients. The dough should be a soft dropping consistency. If it is not, add more milk.

4 Grease a 450g/1lb loaf tin and put the mixture in. Smooth the top and bake for 1 hour or until golden brown and cooked through. Test with a skewer, and when it comes out clean the bread is cooked. Cool on a wire rack.

CHAPTER 4

BERRIES

We are lucky in Britain in being richly endowed with fruits and berries. Dark, juicy brambles are common everywhere, as are sloes and elderberries. Others, such as bilberry, are more unusual, but still there for the picking if you know where to look.

When picking berries, choose fruit away from the roadside, as roadside trees carry a high dosage of lead from exhaust fumes. Be careful not to damage the mother plant and don't stray on to private property without permission. Above all, remember the country code – close gates behind you, keep your dog under control, and don't leave litter.

BLACKBERRIES

Blackberries are the most common of our wild fruit. They flourish in hedgerows, on common land, rough ground, scrub, copse and wood. The dark, juicy berries ripen in late August and throughout September, depending on how sunny the summer has been.

Country people have always valued blackberries, not only to make into jams, jellies and puddings, but also for wines and various home cures. The berries are high in vitamin C, so were often made into teas, cordials and syrups to soothe sore throats and colds. As a child, I was fed blackberry cordial, liberally anointed with goose grease, wrapped in a brown paper vest and confined to bed with hot water bottles and a mound of blankets to drive out bronchitis. My grandmother, who regularly brewed up powerful cordials from fruit, flowers, herbs and ginger, swore it was this smelly, hot, and certainly uncomfortable treatment, and not the penicillin administered by the doctor, that cured me.

Medieval herbalists regarded the leaves and fruit as a cure for a serpent's bite. Today whole plantations of rich, juicy black fruit are left to the birds, but as little as 30 years ago blackberries played an important part in the winter diet of country people. Bushes were stripped of the edible fruit, some was eaten fresh, and the rest turned into jam or jelly, or bottled for winter use. In Cumberland we called blackberries 'blackites'. The village children were regularly dispatched after school or on a Saturday morning to bring enough back for a pie. The big harvest to collect for jam and jelly was left until weekends. The berries were picked as soon as they were ripe. Left too long they became sport for 'Old

Nick' who poisoned the fruit by spitting on it. Old Nick's visit was on Old Holy Rood Day in Scotland (September 26) and on October 10 in the rest of Britain. An old Scottish rhyme warns unwary bramble pickers:

'Oh weans! Oh weans! The morn's the Fair
Ye may na eat the berries mair
This nicht the Deil gangs ower them a'
To touch them with his poisoned paw.'

The date when Old Nick was supposed to call probably goes back to the time when the English calendar was adjusted by 11 days in 1752. October 10 corresponds to September 29, the old date for Michealmas Day when St Michael banished Lucifer from heaven.

A pair of stout gloves and a hooked walking stick are essential accessories for blackberrying expeditions. The stick is used to pull branches from the middle of the bush to within reach, while the gloves protect hands from the thorns.

To freeze raw blackberries pack them in shallow layers in a rigid container, sprinkling a little caster sugar between each layer. To cook and then freeze blackberries toss the berries in caster sugar to taste, leave until the juice has begun to run from the berries and then stew them gently over a low heat until just tender (don't add water). Cool and freeze in convenient quantities.

Blackberry Syrup

Straining time: 12 hours   Cooking time: 1 hour

Blackberry syrup should be kept either in a screw-topped bottle or in one which has a lever-operated top; corked bottles have a tendency to pop. Be sure to sterilise all bottles first. If you have room in your freezer the syrup can be frozen in ice-cube trays and then stored in bags ready for use.

1.5kg/3lb blackberries
Caster sugar

1 Put the berries into a large, heavy-bottomed pan with just over a quarter of a pint of water. Simmer gently for about 1 hour, gently crushing the fruit against the side of the pan at intervals.

2 Strain the fruit through a jelly-bag. Stir in 25g/1oz caster sugar. Keep stirring until the sugar has dissolved. Strain the juice. Allow it to cool and then bottle or freeze.

Serving suggestion: Dilute the syrup with hot water to taste as a soothing cold remedy, or pour it undiluted over ice-cream.

Pickled Spiced Berries

Makes 1.5kg/3lb   Preparation and cooking time: 40 minutes   Storage time: 1 month

Delicious served with cold meats and poultry. Bottle in preserving jars which must be sterilised before use.

1.5kg/3lb ripe blackberries
450g/1lb caster sugar
275ml/½ pint good malt
   vinegar
½ teaspoon ground cloves
½ teaspoon ground cinnamon
½ teaspoon groung nutmeg

1 Mix the vinegar, sugar, and spices together. Simmer for 5 minutes.

2 Add the blackberries. Simmer for a further 15 minutes, until the fruit is just tender. Bottle whilst hot. Keep in a dark place for at least 1 month before use; this allows the flavours to seep through the fruit.

Suffolk Blackberry Cordial

Preparation and standing time: 7 days   Cooking time: 10 minutes
Storage time: 1 month

The recipe for this comforting cordial comes from the windswept
farmlands of Suffolk where it was often served, diluted with hot water, as
a cure for colds and sore throats. An old-fashioned earthenware jar is
still the best container to use, but you can use a rumtopf if you have one.

1kg/2lb 3oz ripe blackberries
575ml/1 pint white vinegar
450g/1lb cube sugar
225g/8oz clear honey

1 Pack the blackberries into the jar, then pour on the vinegar. Cover the
jar and let the mixture stand for 7 days. Press the blackberries down
with a potato masher twice a day to extract all the juice.

2 After 7 days strain the fruit through a jelly-bag into a pan. Stir in the
sugar and honey. Bring slowly to the boil, stirring all the time.
Simmer for 5 minutes.

3 Allow the cordial to cool. Pour into dark brown or green bottles. Cork
and store in a cool, dark place. Keep for at least 1 month before use.

Apple and Blackberry Sponge Pudding

Serves 6   Preparation time: 30 minutes   Conventional cooking time:
35 – 40 minutes

This quick-to-make pudding can be steamed, oven-baked or micro-waved. It freezes well.

For the filling:
225g/8oz cooking apples
    peeled, cored and sliced
225g/8oz blackberries
75g/3oz caster sugar

For the sponge:
100g/4oz self-raising flour
1 teaspoon baking powder
100g/4oz caster sugar
100g/4oz soft margarine
2 eggs, beaten

Steam, bake or microwave (*see* below).

1 Mix the fruits and 75g/3oz sugar together. Leave to stand for 15
  minutes then simmer gently over a low heat for 5 minutes. Line the
  base of a 575ml/1 pint basin or pudding dish with this mixture.

2 Place the sponge ingredients into a dish and whisk together. When
  light and fluffy pile the mixture over the fruit. Level the top, hollowing
  slightly in the centre.

3 To steam, cover the top of the basin with a piece of pleated, greased
  foil. Steam for 1½ hours.

4 To bake in the oven, heat the oven to 180°C/350°F/Gas Mark 4 and
  bake for 35–40 minutes until the sponge is golden.

5 To microwave, cover the top of the pudding with clingfilm. Microwave
  on full power for 7–10 minutes (depending on the power of your
  microwave), until the sponge is well-risen and firm.

Serving suggestion: Serve with custard or cream.

To freeze: Wrap the uncooked pudding in clingfilm. If you want to bake the pudding, thaw first. To steam, cook from frozen for 2 hours. To microwave, cook on the defrost setting for 4 minutes, then continue to cook on full. as above.

Lemony Blackberry Crumble

Serves 6   Preparation time: 20 minutes   Cooking time: 35 minutes

Lemon peel adds a delicious tang to the crumble topping of this pudding. Orange peel can also be used.

450g/1lb ripe blackberries
25g/1oz caster sugar
175g/6oz self-raising flour
Finely grated peel of a lemon
75g/3oz butter
100g/4oz soft brown sugar

Pre-heat the oven to 180°C/350°F/Gas Mark 4

1 Sift the flour into a bowl and rub in the butter until the mixture resembles very coarse crumbs. Stir in the sugar and the grated lemon peel.

2 Put the berries into the base of a 9in/23cm ovenproof dish. Sprinkle on the sugar and stir the fruit in gently. Sprinkle the crumble mixture over the top and press down lightly. Bake for 35 minutes.

Serving suggestion: Serve with custard or cream.

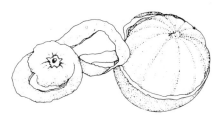

Summer Pudding

Serves 6   Preparation and storage time: 8½ hours

Blackberries are a delicious alternative to blackcurrants in summer pudding. They are particularly good if mixed with raspberries. Thinly sliced white packet bread is best for summer pudding.

450g/1lb blackberries
350g/¾lb raspberries
100g/4oz caster sugar
1 teaspoon lemon juice
10 slices white bread

1 Toss the fruits in the sugar. Leave for 15 minutes and then warm gently in a pan until the juices begin to flow. Remove from the heat.

2 Cut the crusts off the bread. Cut a circle of bread to fit the base of an 850ml/1½ pint basin. Cut another circle to fit the top. Put the first circle in the bottom of the basin, lining the sides with slices of bread, overlapping them slightly.

3 Pile the fruit into the lined basin. Put the top circle of bread in place. Top with a plate which fits just inside the top of the basin and weight it down. Leave in a cool place for at least 8 hours to allow the juice to soak into the bread. Turn the contents out on to a plate.

Serving suggestion: Serve with whipped cream.

Bramble Mousse

Serves 6   Preparation time: 40 minutes   Setting time: 1–2 hours

Blackberries are a very seedy fruit, so the purée must be strained through muslin before it can be made into this delicious foamy mousse.

900g/2lb blackberries
100g/4oz caster sugar
4 teaspoons lemon juice
1 sachet gelatine powder
125ml/4fl oz whipping cream
2 large egg-whites

1 Place the blackberries into a saucepan with the sugar and lemon juice. Toss and leave to stand for 15 minutes.

2 Simmer the fruit over a very low heat for 5 minutes. Purée the fruit in a food processor or blender, then strain it through a muslin-lined sieve.

3 Put 2 tablespoons of cold water into a shallow bowl. Sprinkle the gelatine powder on to the water and leave it to soak for 5 minutes. Warm the gelatine very gently until clear. On no account allow the gelatine to boil, and do not stir it whilst it is melting.

4 Pour the gelatine into the blackberry purée in a thin stream, stirring all the time. Whip the cream until it just holds its shape and then gradually stir the blackberry purée into it.

5 Whisk the egg-whites until stiff. Fold carefully into the blackberry and cream mixture. Turn the mixture into a glass bowl or into individual dishes and leave to set in the refrigerator for 1–2 hours.

Serving suggestion: Decorate with whipped cream, fresh blackberries and curls of lemon rind before serving.

Bramble Jelly

Makes 1.8kg/4lb   Straining time: 12 hours   Cooking time: 1 hour

This is one of the nicest of all home preserves.

1.8kg/4lb blackberries
Juice of 2 lemons
Caster sugar (weight depends
*   on amount of juice after straining)*

1 Put the fruit, lemon juice and 450ml/¾ pint water into a large pan. Simmer over a very low heat for 1 hour until the fruit is pulpy.

2 Strain the pulp through a jelly-bag. This takes about 12 hours but don't try to hurry the process by touching or squeezing the bag as the jelly will become cloudy if you do.

3 Measure the amount of juice and return it to the pan. Add 350g/12oz caster sugar for each 575ml/1 pint of juice. Heat gently, stirring until the sugar has dissolved. Boil to setting point.

4 Pour into hot, sterilised jars and cover.

Note: Use just ripe blackberries for best results. Squashy ones don't give a good flavour.

ROWAN

The glorious red berries of the rowan or mountain ash are one of the most beautiful sights of autumn. Rowan, also known as Quickbeam, Wicken or Witchbeam, is believed to have great powers against the forces of darkness. Dried rowanberries, hung above the door, or better still a whole tree planted in the garden, protects the family, their pets and the house against evil spells.

Walking sticks and farm implements made from rowan wood were believed to be just as effective protectors. Rowan wood used for coffins was thought to keep the dead from walking, and rowan trees were often planted in churchyards, both to protect the dead from evil – and to keep them firmly where they belonged!

Rowan twigs bound with red ribbons were hung above barn doors on

30 April, the eve of the old Celtic festival of Beltane, which marked the beginning of summer, and also on Hallowe'en to protect cattle from evil. Farmers' wives wore a necklace of dried rowanberries if there was a suspected witch in the neighbourhood in order to protect themselves and their farms from the sorceress.

Today, rowanberries are mainly used in autumnal flower arrangements and to make rowan jelly, which is delicious with cold meats, game and poultry.

Rowanberry Jelly

Makes 1.8kg/4lb   Straining time: 12 hours

2kg/4½lb ripe rowanberries
6 tablespoons lemon juice
Caster sugar (the amount
  depends on how much juice
  is left after cooking)

1 Take the rowanberries off their stems and place them in a large, heavy-based pan with 1.1 litres/2 pints water and the lemon juice.

2 Simmer the berries until the fruit is soft. Strain the pulp and liquid through a jelly-bag. This takes about 12 hours. Do not touch the bag during this time.

3 Allow 450g/1lb caster sugar to each 575ml/1 pint of juice. Stir in the sugar over a low heat and keep stirring until the sugar has dissolved.

4 Boil the jelly rapidly until setting point is reached. This is when the jelly registers 105°C/221°F on a sugar thermometer. Cool and store in sterilised jars with covers.

SLOE

The sloe is the fruit of the blackthorn tree. Small, dark and bitter, it looks rather like an undersized plum. In Elizabethan times, the sloe was recommended as a remedy for diarrhoea. In his *Five Hundred Points of Good Husbandry*, 1573, Tusser says:

*'By th' end of October, go gather up sloes
Have thou in readiness plenty of those
And keep them in bedstraw, or still on the bough
To stay both the flux of thyself and thy cow.'*

Sloes are best if picked after the first frost as this makes the skins softer. Sloe gin, a brew with a kick like a horse, is the most popular way to use sloes, and in some parts of Britain it is traditionally served at Christmas.

Blackthorn blossom is thought to be unlucky in some areas. In Cumbria, my mother would never allow even a sprig to enter the house.

Sloe Gin

Storage time: 3 months

450g/1lb sloes
100g/4oz caster sugar
Few drops almond essence
1×75cl bottle London dry gin

1 Wash the sloes and prick the skins at intervals with a darning needle. Put the sloes into a preserving jar with a clamp top or a screw-top.

2 Add the sugar and almond essence. Fill the container with gin and close the top. Shake well and then leave in a dark place for 3 months.

3 At the end of 3 months strain the liquid through muslin until clear. Bottle and keep until required.

Note: Instead of almond essence you can use a little Amaretto di Saronno liqueur for extra kick!

Sloe and Blackberry Jelly

Preparation and straining time: 8–12 hours

2kg/4½lb ripe blackberries
450g/1lb ripe sloes
Caster sugar (weight depends
on amount of juice after straining)

1 Wash the sloes and prick them with a darning needle. Add the blackberries. Cover the fruit with water and simmer over a low heat until tender.

2 Strain the fruit through a jelly-bag. It will take 8–12 hours for the fruit to strain properly.

3 Measure the juice and allow 450g/1lb caster sugar to each 575ml/1 pint of fruit juice. Stir in the sugar over a low heat until dissolved. Boil rapidly until the jelly reaches setting point on a sugar thermometer.

4 Pour into sterilised jars. Cover and store in a dark place.

Sloe Wine

Preparation time: 3 days

2kg/4½lb sloes
50g/2oz root ginger
Caster sugar (weight depends
*   on amount of liquid after*
*   straining)*

1 Wash and prick the sloes with a darning needle. Place them in a large container and pour on 4.5 litres/1 gallon boiling water.

2 Bruise the ginger by hitting it with a rolling pin. Add it to the sloes and cover the container. Leave the liquid for 3 days, stirring daily.

3 Strain the liquid. Add 450g/1lb caster sugar per 1 litre/2 pints of liquid. Stir well to dissolve.

4 Bottle the liquid. Cork it lightly. Corking too tightly means the bottles may explode.

5 Leave the bottles in a dark place until fermentation takes place, i.e. when bubbles rise to the top. The wine can be drunk at this point but tastes better if kept for a while.

CRAB-APPLES

Small, hard and excruciatingly sour, the crab-apple thrives in clay and sandy soils. Also known as Apple-John, Crab-Stock, Morris Apple and Scrog, it can be found in woodland and sometimes in hedgerows. Crab-apple trees were a rarity in my home village; we only ever found two in our forays across the fields and woods. The apples are about the size of a walnut and cannot be mistaken for any other fruit.

The juice of the crab-apple was greatly valued as a treatment for sprains and in Ireland was added to cider to roughen it up. Crabs are usually ripe in September and early October. Their main use is for making a delicious clear green jelly.

Crab-Apple Jelly

Straining time: 12 hours

3kg/6½lb crab-apples
Juice of 1 large lemon
Caster sugar (weight depends
on amount of juice after
straining)

1 Wipe the apples and slice them roughly. Leave in the peel, cores and pips as these help the jelly to set.

2 Place the apples in a pan with 2 litres/3½ pints water and simmer gently until pulpy. Strain through a jelly-bag. This will take at least 12 hours. Do not push the pulp through as this tends to make the jelly cloudy.

3 Stir the sugar into the juice, allowing 450g/1lb of sugar to each 575ml/1 pint liquid. Stir in the lemon juice, and continue stirring over a low heat until the sugar has dissolved. Bring to the boil and continue boiling until setting point is reached on a sugar thermometer.

4 Pour the jelly into warmed, sterilised jars. Store until needed.

Crab-Apple Butter

Preparation time: 30 minutes

This delicious, tangy fruit spread is a pleasant alternative to sweeter jams and preserves.

3kg/6½lb crab-apples
1.1 litres/2 pints water
1.1 litres/2 pints dry cider
1 teaspoon ground cloves
1 teaspoon ground cinnamon
1 teaspoon ground nutmeg
Soft brown sugar (weight
    depends on amount of apple
    pulp after straining)

1 Cut the apples into chunks. There is no need to peel or core the fruit.

2 Simmer the apples in the water and cider until pulpy. Push the pulp through a sieve.

3 Simmer the pulp until it is thick. Weigh the pulp and add 350g/12oz sugar to each 450g/1lb pulp. Stir in the spices.

4 Cook slowly, stirring until there is no surplus liquid. Pour into hot, sterilised jars and cover.

Note: If you can't find enough crab-apples, mix them with orchard apples.

Crab-Apple Chutney

Preparation time: 40 minutes   Cooking time: 40 minutes

This sharp, spicy chutney is good with mildly flavoured meats such as chicken.

1kg/2lb 3oz crab-apples
225g/8oz onions
225g/8oz soft brown sugar
100g/4oz sultanas
1 tablespoon salt
425ml/¾ pint malt vinegar
1 tablespoon pickling spice
½ tablespoon dry English
  mustard powder
1 teaspoon coriander seeds
2 pieces root ginger

1 Peel and core the apples. Mince the apples and onions. Simmer in half of the vinegar until tender.

2 Add the sugar, sultanas, salt, spices, ginger and remaining vinegar. Simmer for 30 minutes or until thick.

3 Take out the pieces of ginger and pour the chutney into warmed jars. Cover. Use either kilner preserving jars with a glass lid, or ordinary jars with a thick layer of waxed paper between the chutney and the metal of the lid.

Crab-Apple and Scented Geranium Jelly

Straining time: 12 hours

Raid the garden for some of the leaves from a scented geranium to make this fragrant jelly. Rose geranium gives the best results.

3 large handfuls of scented
geranium leaves
1½kg/3lb crab-apples
Caster sugar (weight depends
on amount of juice after
straining)

1 Shred the geranium leaves. Cut the apples into chunks, but do not peel or core.

2 Put the fruit and leaves into a pan and cover with water. Simmer until the fruit is soft. Strain through a jelly-bag. This will take about 12 hours and should not be hurried.

3 Add 450g/1lb caster sugar to each 575ml/1 pint juice. Stir over a low heat until the sugar is dissolved. Bring to the boil and simmer until setting point is reached on a sugar thermometer.

4 Pour the jelly into warmed, sterilised jars. Cover and store until needed.

ELDER

The elder bears a double gift for country dwellers. The white flowers which appear in early summer can be used to make heady, effervescent elderflower champagne while the black, juicy autumnal berries can be turned into wines, jellies and cordials.

Old country names for the elder are Pipe Tree, Bore Tree, Hylder and Eldrum. The tree flourishes in hedgerows and on rough ground all over Britain. Despite its pretty flowers and innocent appearance, the elder has a sinister reputation. Elders were rarely cut down, because to cut or burn the tree was believed to stir the wrath of the Elder Mother who lived inside. This belief probably dates back to the pagan worship of the Moon Goddess whose sacred tree was the elder. Elder branches gathered on

May Day, the most mystical day of the Celtic year, were recommended as a cure for the bite of a rabid dog, but the cutter had to remember the following charm to pacify the Elder Mother: 'Old girl, give me of thy wood, and I will give you some of mine when I am earth and turn into a tree.'

Christians believed that the tree was unlucky because Judas Iscariot hanged himself on an elder. As a result, anything made from the wood of an elder carried misfortune with it. Burning elder on the fire calls up the devil who will come and sit on the chimney.

The elder has great medicinal properites. Elderflower water was used liberally as a complexion whitener and freckle-bleacher by ladies of the Regency period, and it is still a good treatment for sunburn. Mrs Harrington, an eighteenth century lady who was the premier 'agony aunt' of her day, recommended the following:

'Water of elder flowers for a pure complexion, and against insect biting. Take the flowers off the stalks and pack them down hard in your pan, then pour on enough water to cover them: cover your pan with a cloth and so let it stand a day and night, and then strain it.'

A mixture of elderflower and peppermint is still used in some country areas as a cure for coughs and colds. Berries, flowers, leaves and bark were all used to treat constipation, arthritis, flu ('the ague'), hay fever, catarrh, bruises, chilblains and sprains. Elderberries should be picked when they have just turned black and are drooping downwards.

Elderflower Champagne

Makes 4 litres/1 gallon   Storage: 4 – 5 days

As children, my friend Liz and I helped my grandmother to make elderflower champagne; explosions were frequent. This particular mixture is less volatile.

8 large elderflower heads with
flowers open
900g/2lb sugar
2 tablespoons white wine
vinegar
2 lemons

1 Place the elderflowers, sugar and vinegar into a 4 litre/1 gallon bucket, or divide between 2 smaller buckets. Fill with cold water.

2 Squeeze the lemons and stir the juice into the elderflower mixture. Chop the lemon skins roughly and add them to the mixture. Cover the bucket and leave the mixture for 24 hours. Stir about half a dozen times.

3 Strain the liquid and place in screw-topped bottles. Keep the bottles in a cool place. The champagne is ready to drink in 4 or 5 days.

Serving suggestion: Elderflower champagne is delicious served with orange juice.

Elderberry Jelly

Makes 1.8kg/4lb   Straining time: 12 hours

900g/2lb elderberries, stalks
*   removed*
900g/2lb cooking apples
Sugar (weight depends on
*   amount of juice after straining)*

1 Chop the apples. Do not peel or core them as the peel and pips help the jelly to set.

2 Place the fruits in 2 large pans; the elderberries and apples must be cooked separately. Add water to cover and simmer until pulpy.

3 Strain the fruits through a jelly-bag. This will probably take several hours but do not try to hurry the process by pushing the fruit through as this makes the jelly cloudy.

4 Measure the juice and weigh out 350g/12oz sugar for each 575ml/1 pint. Add the sugar to the juice and stir well until the sugar has dissolved. Boil rapidly until the jelly has reached setting point on a sugar thermometer.

5 Pour into hot sterilised jars. Cover, and store in a cool, dark place.

Elderberry Chutney

Makes 1kg/2½lb   Preparation time: 30 minutes   Cooking time: 1 hour

Like all chutnies, this is delicious with cold meats and pies.

1 kg/2½lb elderberries, stalks
  removed
1 large onion, skinned and
  chopped
50g/2oz dark soft brown sugar
275ml/½ pint malt vinegar
1 tablespoon ground ginger
6 cloves
1 teaspoon salt
Generous pinch of ground
  black pepper
Generous pinch of mace
Generous pinch of allspice
50g/2oz sultanas and raisins,
  mixed

1 Push the elderberries through a fine sieve to remove the seeds. Put all the ingredients together into a large pan.

2 Simmer over a low heat for about 1 hour until the mixture is thick and cooked through. Allow to cool, then store in sterilised jars.

Elderberry Wine

Makes 3 litres/6 pints   Storage: keeps for up to 2 years

900g/2lb elderberries
Pectin enzyme
Wine yeast
1 packet campden tablets
1.5kg/3¼lb sugar

1 Pull the berries off the stalks and crush roughly. Put them into a strong plastic container with 1.3 litres/2½ pints of boiling water and the campden tablets, which can be bought from any wine-making shop. Cover and leave overnight.

2 Add 2 litres/4 pints of warmed water, the pectin enzyme and the wine yeast. Put the mixture into a wine demijohn and fit an airlock. Leave for 3 days.

3 Strain the liquid and return it to a clean demijohn. Fit an airlock and leave the jar to ferment in a warm place. Fermentation should cease after about 6 weeks. Siphon the wine into a clean demijohn fitted with an airlock and leave it to clear.

4 Bottle the wine and keep for up to 2 years in a cool, dark place.

Note: Pectin enzyme can be bought at any home wine-making shop.

Elderberry Syrup

Straining time: 12 hours   Cooking time: 4 hours

Elderberry syrup is very good for colds. Dilute it to taste with hot water, and add a few drops of peppermint for a different flavour.

2kg/4½lb elderberries
(weighed after removing
stalks)
1 small egg-white
Sugar (weight depends on
amount of juice after
straining)
Brandy to taste

1 Wash the berries. Put them into an ovenproof pot with 575ml/1 pint water. Leave in a very low oven until the fruit is squashy. This may take 3–4 hours.

2 Strain the fruit through a jelly-bag. Weigh out 450g/1lb sugar per 575ml/1 pint of juice, and place to one side.

3 Whisk the egg-white so that it is frothy but not stiff. Put the juice in a pan and add the egg-white. Bring the juice to the boil and skim off the scum.

4 Warm the sugar gently in the oven and add it to the juice. Bring the liquid to the boil and simmer for 5 minutes, skimming off scum as it rises. Add the brandy to taste and store in heated, sterilised bottles. Seal the bottles tightly.

HAWTHORN

Hawthorn leaves are almost the first to be seen in spring and are a welcome sign that lighter, warmer days are on the way. The young leaves have a delicious, nutty flavour — country children call them 'bread and cheese' and eat them straight from the tree. They are delicious in salads, but pick them from a tree well away from traffic fumes. The leaves are followed by highly-scented pink and white blossoms, with bright red berries in the autumn.

Hawthorn is sacred in both pagan religion and Christianity. In pre-Christian days the tree was associated with fertility goddesses and fairies. The early Christian church believed that hawthorn was used for the crown of thorns worn by Christ at the crucifixion and that the very first hawthorn tree in Britain grew at Glastonbury from the staff of Joseph of Aramathea.

Like blackthorn, hawthorn blossom is held to be very unlucky and it is believed that it should never be picked and brought into the house before May Day. This may be because country people believed that hawthorn blossom carried the smell of the Great Plague. After May Day, the hawthorn changed its spots and could be laid above the door lintel to ward off witches, hobgoblins and lightning. Such was the power of hawthorn against tempest that country folk believed it was safe to stand beneath a hawthorn tree during a thunderstorm as its magical properies would protect those sheltering from lightning:

'*Beware of the oak*
It draws the smoke
Around the ash
It courts the flash
Creep under the thorn
It will save you from harm.'

The old name for hawthorn is May – hence the old saying 'ne'er cast a clout 'till May be out', referring to the blossoming of the hawthorn tree rather than the month of May. Medieval maidens bathed in the dew from hawthorn trees at dawn on May Day:

'A fair maid who, the first of May,
Goes to the fields at break of day
And washes in the dew from the hawthorn tree
Will ever after handsome be'.

My friend Liz and I took this greatly to heart and carried on performing the early morning May Day ritual until we reached the age when staying in bed seemed a more attractive prospect than the uncertain promise of good looks for life.

Hawthorn berries (or cat haws as we called them) infused in boiling water were once used to treat heart disease.

Spring Salad

Preparation time: 10 minutes

Young hawthorn and
* dandelion leaves*
Curly endive
Oak leaf lettuce
Radiccio
Crisply fried bacon
Croûtons
Walnut oil
Chopped walnuts

1 The amount of each ingredient allowed depends on the number of people you are serving. As a rough guide, allow a handful of mixed hawthorn and dandelion, a handful of salad leaves, one bacon rasher, 1 tablespoon crôutons, 1 tablespoon of walnut oil and several walnuts per person.

2 Wash the leaves and toss with the bacon and walnuts, together with the walnut oil. Sprinkle with croûtons, and serve immediately.

Hawthorn Jelly

Straining time: 12 hours

This jelly is good served with cold meat, especially game.

1.5kg/3lb hawthorn berries
Juice of 3 lemons
Sugar (the weight depends on
*   the amount of juice after*
*   straining)*

1 Pick the berries when they are a deep red. Wash them and put into a large pan with 1 litre/2 pints of water. Simmer the fruit over a low heat until it is tender, mashing the fruit occasionally.

2 Strain the pulp through a jelly-bag. This will take several hours but do not try to push the fruit through as this makes the jelly cloudy.

3 Allow 450g/1lb of sugar for each 575ml/1 pint of liquid. Stir in the sugar and lemon juice then bring the liquid to the boil. Boil until it reaches setting point on a sugar thermometer. Pour into heated jars, cover and store.

ROSE-HIP

Brilliant scarlet rose-hips are the fruit of the dog rose, Rupert Brooke's 'English unofficial rose'. The name dog rose comes from the medieval belief that the flower was a cure for the bite of a rabid dog. Maidens were also advised to pick a pink or red dog rose on Midsummer Eve. If the flower had not faded by the beginning of the next month, the girl knew her lover was faithful.

Rose-hips are a valuable source of vitamin C and used in many old remedies to treat colds. During World War II and in the 1950s when oranges were in short supply and expensive, rose-hip syrup was manufactured in vast quantities. The makers paid schoolchildren 4d per pound for the hips, which had to be topped, tailed and washed. Anyone collecting 10lb was given a rose-hip badge – a much-prized status symbol. To us country children 4d per pound was big money and we ranged the hedgerows for miles around during the rose-hip season. Some large families had rose-hip syndicates with everyone from the smallest toddler to Grandad out collecting. My dad was almost as enthusiastic as I and would drive as far as the lanes around Cockermouth, well out of reach of my Arlecdon schoolfellows, in search of new and better hedges.

It was poetic justice that the most hated school pudding was either rice or semolina (which looked and tasted like wallpaper paste) with a dollop of rose-hip syrup in the middle. None of us could ever face it in the rose-hip season.

Rose-Hip Syrup

Makes 1.8 litres/3 pints   Straining time: 12 hours   Cooking time: 10 minutes

1kg/2lb 3oz rose-hips
600g/1¼lb sugar

1 Top and tail the rose-hips then mince the fruit. Put it into a large pan with 1.8 litres/3 pints of boiling water. Bring the liquid to the boil then remove it from the heat and leave to stand for 15 minutes.

2 Strain the fruit through a jelly-bag. This will take 12 hours or more. Don't force it through or the syrup will become cloudy.

3 Place the strained juice in a pan with the sugar. Stir over a low heat until the sugar has dissolved. Boil for 5 minutes. Bottle the syrup in sterilised bottles and store.

Serving suggestion: Use the syrup with ice-creams and puddings, or diluted in hot water as a soothing drink for colds and sore throats.

Rose-Hip Jelly

Straining time: 12 hours

Rose-hip jelly is good with poultry and game. The hips should be very ripe and slightly soft for jelly making.

1kg/2½lb rose-hips
Sugar (weight depends on
    amount of juice after straining)

1 Roughly chop the hips. Put them into a large pan with just enough water to cover. Bring to the boil. Reduce the heat and simmer until the hips are pulpy.

2 Strain through a jelly-bag. This takes about 12 hours. Do not try to hurry it as this makes the jelly cloudy.

3 Allow 450g/1lb of sugar to each 575ml/1 pint of juice. Stir the sugar into the juice. Stir over a low heat until all the sugar has dissolved. Boil until the liquid reaches setting point on a sugar thermometer.

4 Pour into warmed sterilised jars and store.

BILBERRY

Bilberries grow on fells, heath and moorland. Sometimes called the whinberry, the bilberry grows on low, bushy plants. The berries are small and a deep purple colour. Picking them is hard work. Bilberries can be used to make jelly, jams, pies and puddings. The juice is used in the Hebrides as a natural dye for tweeds.

Bilberry Pie

Serves 4   Preparation time: 30 minutes   Cooking time: 30 minutes

Bilberry pie was a great autumn treat when I was a child. It was served either hot or cold with thick, whipped cream.

225g/8oz shortcrust pastry
450g/1lb bilberries
150g/5oz caster sugar

Pre-heat the oven to 200°C/400°F/Gas Mark 6

1 Roll out half the pastry and cut a round to fit the base of a 20cm/8in shallow pie plate. Line the plate with the pastry.

2 Toss the fruit with the sugar. Place in the dish and top with the remaining pastry rolled out to fit. Brush with beaten egg.

3 Bake the pie for 15 minutes, then reduce the heat to 180°C/350°F/Gas Mark 4 for a further 15 minutes.

Bilberry Jam

Makes 2½kg/5½lb   Straining time: 12 hours

Apples and lemon juice are used to help this jam to set.

2kg/4½lb bilberries
450g/1lb cooking apples
2kg/4½lb sugar
Juice of 1 lemon

1 Peel, core and slice the apples. Place them in a preserving pan. Add about a cupful of water and simmer them gently until the apples are pulpy.

2 Strain the apples through a jelly-bag. Put the bilberries into a pan with the lemon juice. Simmer over a low heat until soft.

3 Add the apple juice and the sugar. Boil until the jam reaches setting point on a sugar thermometer. Pour into warmed, sterilised jars.

CRANBERRY

If you look carefully on the high mossy fells and peat bogs of northern England and Scotland you may be lucky enough to find the delicious wild cranberry. These bright scarlet berries grow low on the ground in clumps. They are juicy and full of flavour, a vivid contrast to the dull cultivated cranberry available in supermarkets. Cranberries are ripe in the autumn.

Cranberry and Orange Conserve

Makes 225g/8oz Preparation and standing time: 1½ hours

Serve this as a special treat with the Christmas turkey. It is also very good with lamb, venison and game.

225g/8oz cranberries
Grated rind and juice of 1
  orange
Juice of 1 lemon
150g/5oz caster sugar
Sachet of gelatine

1 Toss the cranberries with the sugar and leave to stand for 1 hour.

2 Add the orange rind, most of the orange juice and the lemon juice. Simmer gently until the berries are tender. Dissolve the gelatine in a little orange juice. Stir into the fruit well. Pour into sterilised, warmed jars and store.

Cranberry Sauce

Makes 450g/1lb Preparation time: 15 minutes Cooking time: 10 minutes

This is a traditional accompaniment to turkey and game but is also good with lamb.

450g/1lb cranberries
100g/4oz sugar
2 wine glasses vintage port

1 Put the cranberries into a pan with 1 wine glass of water and simmer until they are soft. Push through a sieve.

2 Stir in the sugar and re-heat until dissolved. Stir in the port. The sauce will keep in a sealed jar in the refrigerator for up to 1 month.

WILD STRAWBERRIES

The tiny, sweet wild strawberry can be found nestling on banks, in steep hedgerows and in woodland glades. It is ripe from late June through to August. The powered hedge-trimmer has made the strawberry a much rarer plant than it was in my own childhood in the 1950s. At that time there were strawberries in an almost unbroken line of hedgerow from the village of Asby to Lamplugh over a mile away. Today there are scarcely any at all. As children we would thread the fruit on to stalks of Timothy grass and take them home to eat with the top of the milk and a sprinkling of sugar. Today it is difficult to find sufficient wild strawberries to be of any great culinary use, but you may be lucky enough to find sufficient berries to make a small pot of preserve, or to serve with creamy cheese (*see* opposite).

Wild Strawberry Conserve

Makes 100g/4oz   Preparation time: Overnight

100g/4oz wild strawberries
100g/4oz sugar

1 Toss the strawberries in the sugar and leave them overnight.

2 Put them into a small pan and bring gently to the boil. Boil for 4 minutes. Leave to stand until cool.

3 Boil again to setting point on a sugar thermometer. Pour into a small warmed pot, seal and cover.

Wild Strawberries and Creamy Cheese

Serves 4   Preparation time: Overnight

Yoghurt cheese is mild, delicious and easy to make. Cream cheeses and sharp fruit .are a classic combination. You can eke out the wild strawberries with blackberries, raspberries or other soft fruit.

For the yoghurt cheese:
275ml/½ pint natural yoghurt
100g/4oz curd cheese
Caster sugar to taste

For the sauce:
225g/8oz strawberries
4 tablespoons orange juice
Icing sugar to taste

To decorate:
Wild strawberries and other
  fruit as available

1 Put the yoghurt into a piece of butter muslin, tie the top and suspend it over a bowl. Leave to drip for 4 – 6 hours, until the yoghurt is thick and cheese-like.

2 Mix the strained yoghurt with the curd cheese and flavour to taste with caster sugar. Pack into heart moulds lined with muslin and leave overnight in the refrigerator.

3 Purée the 225g/8oz strawberries in a blender. Strain through a muslin-lined sieve to get rid of the seeds. Stir in the orange juice and flavour to taste with icing sugar.

4 Pour a pool of sauce on to each serving plate. Turn each cheese heart out on to the centre of the plate. Decorate with the wild strawberries and other fruit.

Wild Strawberry Romanoff

Stir as many wild strawberries as you have into thickly-whipped cream flavoured with brandy.

WILD RASPBERRIES

Wild raspberries are less common than blackberries, but not quite as hard to find as strawberries. They grow in hedges and thickets and are ripe in the autumn.

Village midwives encouraged women in labour to drink raspberry leaf tea to make birth easier – a custom later proved by modern medicine as raspberry leaves contain fragarine which relaxes the pelvic muscles. Raspberry vinegar, which has recently enjoyed a fashionable revival as an ingredient in nouvelle cuisine dishes was used for feverish colds and sore throats. In medieval Europe hunters would use raspberries as bait for bears who could not resist the juicy fruit.

Raspberry Vinegar

Makes 1 pint   Preparation and straining time: 5 days   Cooking time: 20 minutes

450g/1lb raspberries
575ml/1 pint white wine
    vinegar
Sugar to taste

1 Brush the raspberries clean but do not crush them. Pour the vinegar on to the fruit and stir.

2 Cover the container and leave for 3–4 days, stirring now and then. Strain through a jelly-bag. Add sugar to taste.

3 Heat to just below boiling and simmer for 10–15 minutes. Bottle when cold.

4 Use the vinegar diluted in a little lemonade for cooking.

JUNIPER

Juniper can be found in areas where the soil is chalky. The small, dark berries are one of the principal ingredients of gin. The berries are used as a spice in patés and other meat dishes in Britain. In Germany, they are used in sauerkraut, in Sweden in beer and in Lapland as a tea.

Juniper was used as a charm to keep away witches and the plague. Branches were hung over the door of the house on the eve of May Day and a juniper fire was burnt to deter demons. To dream of a juniper tree is considered unlucky, but dreaming of the berries can be a good omen.

The berries themselves are green in their first year and turn black in the second. They are ready to be picked when they are black. Collect the berries and allow them to dry naturally before using in patés and other meat dishes.

CHAPTER 5
HERBS

AGRIMONY

Agrimony grows in hedgerows, on banks and in copses. It has small yellow flowers and can usually be found in July or August. It can't be used in recipes but does have great medicinal properties. My grandmother swore by agrimony poultices for insect bites and stings but she called the plant sticklewort. This belief in the healing cures of agrimony probably dates back to the time when an agrimony poultice was applied to musket wounds.

In medieval times, agrimony was used as a cure for insomnia: 'If agrimony be leyd under a mann's hede he shall slepe as if he were dede. He shall never waken till from under his hede it be taken.' Agrimony flowers are still used in herb pillows. An infusion of agrimony is beneficial to the liver, kidneys and bladder as it acts as a diuretic. To make an infusion of agrimony, pour 150ml/¼ pint of hot water on to half a teaspoon of dried agrimony leaves. Leave to infuse for 15 minutes.

ANGELICA

Angelica, sometimes called Holy Ghost or Archangel, traditionally comes into flower on 8 May, St Michael's Day, although in most years it appears later than this. It can be found in shady, damp places and can grow as high as 1.5m/5 feet. The flowers are large, white and rather like a lacy umbrella. As St Michael is guardian of the gates of heaven, his plant was believed to have great powers against the forces of darkness. Londoners chewed pieces of angelica root during the terrifying days of the Great Plague to protect themselves from infection.

Both the stem and the seeds of angelica are used in cookery. The stem, which is ribbed and hollow, is candied and used for cake decorations and in confectionery. As children we used them as a weapon of war – a big angelica stem makes a wonderful pea-shooter! The seeds are used to make drinks such as anisette and green Chartreuse. Angelica is grown commercially in France.

A teaspoon of dried, crushed angelica seeds in a cup of boiling water is good for feverish colds, headaches, rheumatism and cystitis.

Candied Angelica

Preparation time: 9 days

Real candied angelica is quite unlike the artificial bright green substance sold as a substitute for cake decoration. It is nice enough to eat on its own and makes a lovely Christmas gift packed in a pretty jar.

Young angelica stems
100g/4oz salt
700g/1½lb granulated sugar

1 Cut the angelica stems into 10cm/4in lengths. Put them in a shallow layer in a bowl.

2 Mix the salt with enough boiling water to cover the angelica. Pour over and leave for 24 hours.

3 Lift out the pieces of angelica. Peel them and put in cold water.

4 Mix the sugar with 575ml/1 pint water. Boil for 10 minutes, stirring now and then.

5 Put the angelica pieces into the syrup and boil for 20 minutes. Lift out and leave to drain on a rack for 4 days. Reserve the syrup.

6 Boil the angelica pieces again in the syrup. Leave them to cool in the syrup. Lift out and drain for a further 4 days on a wire rack. Toss the pieces in caster sugar and store them in an airtight container.

Serving suggestion: Candied angelica is very good added to rhubarb tart, crumble or jam.

ALEXANDERS

If you live near the great salt lands of Suffolk and Norfolk or the Medway, you may well have eaten Alexanders. This is one of the earliest plants of the year to appear, with bright, glossy green leaves showing as early as February. By April the plant is 90–120cm/3–4 feet in height with umbrella-shaped greenish-yellow flowers.

Alexanders smell strongly of celery, so the stalk has been widely used as a vegetable. Cut the stalks close to the ground before the flowers appear (they are too woody after this). Peel the stalks and cook them in the same way as asparagus. Serve with butter or Hollandaise sauce. The young leaves of Alexanders can be used in salads and sandwiches.

AVENS

More popularly known as Herb Bennet or St Benedict's Herb, yellow-flowered avens grows in hedges and ditches. It flowers from May to July. The plants grow to about 30cm/1 foot in height and have hairy leaves and small yellow flowers. Avens was an important medicinal plant and useful too as a charm against evil. The leaves grow in threes and the flowers have five petals, so avens was associated with the Holy Trinity and the five wounds of Christ on the cross. It is strongly aromatic, which may have contributed to the belief that carrying a sprig of avens was a sure protection against the bite of a rabid dog or snake. Water from the boiled root is recommended as a cure for catarrh, colds and vomiting.

William Turner, in his herbal of 1568, recommended avens for those suffering from acne:

'The stalk of Herb Bennet is round, all hairy and rough, the flower is in some form like a little eye; when the flower is gone their riseth up a great knob all full of little round things like berries of a purple colour. The common property or use of this root is such that if men put it into wine, it maketh it pleasant both in smelling and taste. Many new writers hold the wine wherein this herb is steeped refresheth the heart and maketh it merry. The same wine scoureth out foul spots if the face be washed daily therewith.'

BALM

Sweet lemon-scented balm is one of the nicest of our wild plants. A sprig is a lovely addition to long summer drinks such as Pimms and it can be used as a culinary herb in salads. Although balm is widely cultivated as a garden herb, it can still be found growing wild in hedgerows and ditches. It is tall with bright green leaves, and is easily identified because of the pungent lemon scent given off when the leaves are crushed. Bees love the yellowish-white flowers of balm, so beekeepers often plant some close to hives, resulting in a honey that is faintly lemon-flavoured.

As well as being used for medicinal purposes, as a soothing drink for sore throats and colds, balm was added to beeswax furniture polish to give it a lemon scent, and mixed with the floor rushes used on castle floors in the Middle Ages.

Balm and Butterbean Salad

Serves 4   Preparation time: 10 minutes

Canned butterbeans gain an interesting new flavour when mixed with onion and fresh balm leaves.

225g/8oz butterbeans
1 medium onion, skinned and
    chopped
1 tablespoon olive oil
2 tablespoons lemon juice
Grated peel of half a lemon
Freshly ground black pepper
2 tablespoons chopped balm
    leaves

1 Empty the butterbeans from the tin and wash them under cold running water. Drain well.

2 Mix the beans with the chopped onions. Put the oil, lemon juice, lemon peel and black pepper into a bowl and mix thoroughly.

3 Toss the beans and onions in the salad dressing. Sprinkle with fresh balm leaves and stir together gently.

Lemon Shrub

Preparation and standing time: 5 days

A shrub in this case is a long, cooling drink, perfect for hot summer days. The word comes from the Arab word shurb, meaning drink. Smith, in his word book of 1667, took an entirely different view: 'a vile drugged drink prepared for seamen who frequent the filthy purlieus of Calcutta.'

70cl bottle brandy (choose a
   cheap brand)
Peel of 2 lemons
Juice of 1 lemon
Handful of balm leaves
½ bottle dry white wine
50g/2oz caster sugar

1 Put the brandy, the lemon peel and lemon juice into a large jug. Gently bruise the balm leaves and add to the jug. Cover and leave to stand for 3 days.

2 Add the wine and sugar and stir well. Cover again and leave in a warm place for 2 days.

3 Strain through muslin, bottle and seal.

Serving suggestion: Drink Lemon Shrub alone with ice, a twist of lemon and a sprig of fresh balm, or mix with lemonade or tonic like Pimms.

BETONY

Although betony has no culinary use, it is worth picking as a charm against the forces of evil, snakebites, sorcery and rabid dogs! Superstition says that two snakes placed within a ring of betony will fight to the death. We tried it once with grass snakes but all they did was ignore each other. Betony was planted in churchyards to prevent the dead from walking. Take a sprig with you should you visit a graveyard at night, especially on Hallowe'en or Midsummer Eve.

BISTORT

When I was a child in Cumbria, the appearance of bistort and the excitements of Easter were firmly linked. Bistort, Easter Ledge, or Eastermun Giant as we called it, was a principal ingredient in herb pudding, a dish always served on Easter Sunday. Herb pudding consists of rhubarb stalks, nettle leaves, spring green cabbage, pearl barley, leeks, oatmeal and eggs. The plants were chopped up, mixed with the barley (soaked overnight), then boiled in a pudding cloth. After boiling, the oatmeal was stirred in and the mixture bound together with a beaten egg. It sounds awful but it tastes delicious. Very few people make herb pudding these days but it is well worth the effort.

BROOM

The growing yellow flowers of broom brighten heathlands and sandy places all over Britain. Broom was the flower of the Plantagenet Kings; Henry II always wore a sprig in his helmet when at war so that he could be recognised by his troops. The flower has a sinister reputation, accounting perhaps for the belief that the Plantagenets were associated with witchcraft. The plant's reputation for evil may also be linked with the old belief that Mary and Joseph cursed the broom when they fled from King Herod, as the crackling of its dry pods as they passed by them risked drawing the attention of his soldiers.

The strong smell of broom is said to calm wild horses and rabid dogs. Broom twigs were once used for sweeping – hence its name. In some counties, sweeping with broom is believed to bring death and disaster to the house, especially during the month of May. The old rhyme says:

'If you sweep the house with broom in May,
You'll sweep the head of the house away.'

Before hops were introduced, the tender young buds of broom were used to add bitterness to beer. They are good added to salad but must be picked early. Old broom is bitter and unpleasant. Be careful when picking broom to use the English rather than the Spanish variety, as Spanish broom is poisonous. It flowers later than English broom and has narrow pine needle-like leaves.

BURDOCK

In the 1950s, when Coca Cola was as exotic to Cumbrian children as fine wine, Dandelion and Burdock, as made by Brothwell and Mills in Workington, was our favourite drink. The bottle has a particularly fetching label, adorned with a large, flourishing burdock and lush dandelion leaves of a highly unlikely green.

Burdock, the principal ingredient in this elixir, is a rough, tough-looking plant, which can grow to about 120cm/4ft high. It flourishes on wasteland and has large, spade-shaped leaves. The flowers, which appear in July, are globe-shaped with purple spikes. Eventually, this flower turns into a collection of very spiky burrs.

Burdock roots can be boiled like parsnips and are delicious served with butter. The young leaves can be chopped up and used in salads. The young stems can be stripped and cooked like asparagus. Burdock is good for purifying the blood. The following recipe is the nearest I have ever come to reproducing the Dandelion and Brudock of my childhood. The real recipe remains a dark secret − though whether Mr Brothwell and Mr Mills were banned from travelling together (like the executives of Coca Cola) in case the formula was lost forever, I shall never know.

Dandelion and Burdock

Preparation and storage time: 11 days   Cooking time: 25 minutes

As the roots of dandelion and burdock are used to make this drink, be prepared to do some digging. For the best flavour, collect the roots in spring.

3 large burdock roots
2 dandelion roots
450g/1lb sugar
2 tablespoons black treacle
1 large lemon
1 sachet yeast

1 Scrub the roots clean. Chop them into small pieces. Boil for 25 minutes in 2.2 litres/4 pints water.

2 Start the yeast, following the instructions on the sachet. Add the sugar and treacle to the roots and water, stirring to dissolve.

3 Add the juice of the lemon. Strain the mixture and add 2.2 litres/ 4 pints more water. When almost cool add the yeast. The liquid should be at blood temperature, 98.4°F/36.9°C.

4 Leave to ferment for about 5 days, then bottle. Screw-topped bottles are best. Release the tops for a couple of seconds every day to prevent the danger of explosion. The brew is ready to drink after a week.

APPENDIX

MAKING JAMS AND JELLIES

Home-made jams and jellies are absolutely delicious, but to ensure a good set and fruity flavour certain rules should be followed.

Don't make the mistake of thinking that any old fruit can be used. The fruit should be sound and either just ripe or slightly under-ripe; over-ripe fruit spoils the flavour of the jam.

Jam will only set naturally if the fruit used is high in pectin, a natural setting agent. If the fruit used has a low pectin content then a setting agent, such as lemon juice or bottled pectin, must be used. If you use bottled pectin, follow the manufacturer's instructions; when using lemon juice follow the instructions given in the recipe you are using.

Sugar acts as a preservative and affects the set of the jam. The amount of sugar used will depend on the amount of pectin in the fruit so always use the amount specified in the recipe, even if you think it may make the jam sweeter than you would like. Honey or a low-calorie sweetner should not be used as a substitute for sugar, as neither of these help the jam to set.

You can buy special preserving sugar for use in jam making, but ordinary granulated is just as good. The only advantage in using preserving sugar is that very little scum is formed on the top of the jam during boiling and the end result is clearer. You can use brown sugar instead of white but the jam will be darker and the flavour of the brown sugar will mask the flavour of the fruit.

Testing for a Set

By far the most accurate way to test if jam is set is to use a sugar thermometer, which can be bought in cookware shops and at hardware stores. The thermometer stays in the pan (it hooks on to the edge) during boiling, and when it registers 105°C setting point has been reached.

As the pectin content of fruit varies it is a good idea to back up the sugar thermometer with the 'saucer test'. When you think the jam has boiled for long enough put a little on to a cold saucer, leave it to cool, then push gently with your finger. If the surface of the jam wrinkles, it has reached setting point. Always remove the jam pan from the heat when carrying out the saucer test. If jam is over-boiled it does not set well.

Potting

There are a few points to observe when potting the jam.

1 Never pour hot jam into cold jars, as the jars will shatter. Sterilise the jars using hot water first, and keep them hot by standing them in a sink of hot water, or in a low oven.
2 Skim the scum from the jam before potting. If you don't do this, the jam will be cloudy.
3 Leave whole fruit jam to settle for 20 minutes or so before potting, otherwise all the fruit will rise to the top.
4 Spoon the jam into the prepared jars. Top with a waxed disc when the jar is full, then cover with cellophane jam pot covers. Remember to label the jars.
5 Store the jars in a cool, dark place. Most jams keep for around a year.

Jam Problems

Sometimes, jam doesn't work out quite as expected. The reasons are simple.

Mould is usually caused because the jam was not covered with a waxed disc as soon as the pot was filled. The other possibility is that the pots were not cleaned and sterilised properly. Don't eat jam with mould growing on the top.

Bubbles are caused by fermentation. This happens if the jam was not boiled for long enough, or if the sugar content was too low.

Crystallisation is caused by either under- or over-boiling the jam after adding the sugar.

Jelly

Jelly is a much trickier product to make than jam. In jelly making only the juice of the fruit is used, and only fruits with a high pectin content are really successful.

Fruit for jelly making should be in good condition. There is no need to peel it, simply wash and chop it into rough pieces.

Always use the amount of water stated in the recipe and cook the fruit slowly and carefully to extract as much juice as possible. When the fruit is cooked (follow the time given in the recipe), pour it into a jelly-bag, which should be scalded before use. The best way to set a jelly-bag is to hook the corner tapes to the four legs of an inverted stool or chair and position a clean bowl beneath it. Leave the juice to drip slowly through the jelly-bag; don't attempt to hurry things up by stirring the contents of the bag as this will make the jelly cloudy.

The amount of sugar used in jelly recipes depends on the amount of juice after straining. The rule is to add 450g/1lb sugar for each 575ml/1 pint of juice from fruits very high in pectin, and 350g/12oz per 575ml/1 pint for medium pectin fruit.

Stir the sugar into the fruit gently then boil the sugared juice for about 10 minutes,. and test for setting in the same way as described for jams. Skim and pot the jelly as for jam.

INDEX